DOMESTIC VIOLENCE

SURVIVOR'S STORIES

BIG BOYS DON'T CRY

KEN BUTLER

Primix Publishing
East Brunswick Office Evolution
1 Tower Center Boulevard, Ste 1510
East Brunswick, NJ 08816
www.primixpublishing.com
Phone: 1-800-538-5788

Published by Primix Publishing: 05/20/2025

ISBN: 979-8-89194-312-4(sc)
ISBN: 979-8-89194-494-7(hc)
ISBN: 979-8-89194-313-1(e)

Library of Congress Control Number: 2024920570

PRIMIX
PUBLISHING
THE WRITE CHOICE

The meaning of life is hard to discover
until you live a life that has meaning to you.
— Ken Butler

"Hope is always a choice at your own fingertips."

Thank you to my wife, who is my "heart and soul."

Thank you to our sons, EJ and TY. Finish well, boys, and be the best you can be.

Thank you to my family members, close friends, trusted colleagues, teachers, and mentors that encouraged me to write about my journey..

Thank you to my tae kwon do teacher for seeing the potential in me and providing me with life lessons that go far beyond kicking and punching.

This book is dedicated to all my siblings, who inspired and moti- vated me to become the man I am today. I have learned so much from everyone in so many different ways. Love, Boo Boo.

1. Gus taught me self-worth.
2. Rosemary taught me how to laugh.
3. Lois taught me how to be a better brother.
4. Butch taught me to never trust anyone 100 percent.
5. Norma taught me how to push myself.
6. Doris taught me how to be calm.
7. David taught me how to never give up.
8. Kenny taught me how to love myself.
9. Robert taught me to stick up for myself.
10. Barbara taught me the power of forgiveness.

Dedication

In all my years growing up, I was always the one leaning on my mother's shoulder. That's why this last photo of us stands frozen in time - just forty-eight hours before we lost her, she rested her head on my shoulder for the first time in my life. Many wish for one final moment to say goodbye. I was blessed with two.

The first came through that photograph on Tuesday. The second arrived Wednesday, when Mother visited my home. Her hug lingered longer than usual that day, held a bit tighter, as if she knew. By Thursday morning, she had quietly slipped away while sitting at the table I gave her, in what I now think of as her chair.

For years, I could only see it as the chair where she died. But time has a way of shifting our perspective. Now I see it as the chair where she truly lived - where she held court for countless hours, nurturing three generations of our family. From this sturdy perch, she shared wisdom with her children, delighted her grandchildren with stories, and cradled her great-grandchildren. More than just furniture, it became her throne of quiet influence, where she taught us all how to stand on our own while remaining rooted in family.

Today, I sit in that same chair to write this book. Its back still hold the warmth of her presence, and within its embrace, I find both comfort

and inspiration. Like Mother herself, this chair represents the foundation of a good home - solid, supportive, always ready to catch us when we falter. Every word of this book has flowed from this sacred space, guided by her enduring spirit of strength and love.

For our wonderful mother, who showed us that true strength lies not just in being a support for others, but in knowing when to lean on those you love.

Elizabeth Chase Butler
June 7, 1921 to June 9, 2011

Contents

I was born in San Diego on November 20, 1961, and moved to Rhode Island six months later. My life has been mostly good - great friends, solid family, worthwhile experiences. But there were some rough patches too. Really rough ones. The kind that stick with you decades later, even when you think you've moved past them.

For years, people kept telling me I should write a book. You know that saying about everyone having a book in them? Well, here's mine. I've picked twenty-five moments that matter, starting from when I was six. Some are obvious turning points - like the day I decided to leave a secure job to start my own business. Others seemed small when they happened but ended up changing everything. A conversation at a bus stop. A wrong turn that led somewhere right. A mistake that turned into an opportunity.

While writing this, I found myself sharing painful things I'd never told anyone before, not even my wife. Some memories are like that - you tuck them away until something makes you pull them out and look at them again. Writing these stories down made me realize why I kept some of them quiet for so long, and why it matters to finally tell them now.

I'm not here to tell you what to learn from my experiences or how they might relate to your life. These are just my stories, told straight. Take from them what you will.

The trouble with society is trauma gauged. Just know that your trauma is valued the same to those who care. When I hear someone say "What's the big deal, get over it ." I always speak up and express the danger in minimizing others trauma. Be kind.

Pictures can paint one thousand words; memories can paint a panorama that is hard to remove from your view.

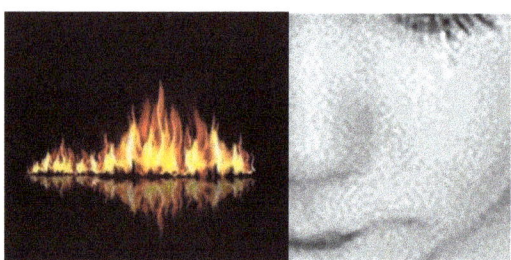

CHAPTER 1

Burning Down the House in Whiskey Land!

The scars of childhood rarely heal in straight lines. In our house, they followed the erratic paths of our father's drunken rages—paths that often led to fire. Though he was a skilled mason who had built every fireplace in our home with his own hands, he didn't always choose to contain his flames within their brick- and-mortar bounds. The fires he started while we slept were like his anger: unpredictable, uncontained, and fueled by whiskey.

Our house was perpetually cold - not just emotionally barren but physically frigid. Despite the fireplaces he had masterfully crafted, my father refused to spend money on proper heating. We lived in a bitter chill that seeped into our bones, making his unpredictable fires both terrifying and, in some perverse way, the only source of warmth we knew.

My mother developed her own ritual in response to his nighttime dangers. Each night, after my father finally collapsed onto the couch in an alcoholic stupor, she would take her position on the floor beside him. It wasn't comfort she sought on that hardwood surface—it was strategy. If he stirred in the night with thoughts of fire or violence, he would have to stumble over her first. Her body became our first warning system, our first line of defense, as she lay shivering on the cold floor through the night.

I was five years old when one of those warnings came too late. The memory starts with sound: heavy thuds and shouting that cut through the darkness of our shared bedroom, where my bed lay tucked beneath the twins' crib. As I crawled out from my makeshift sanctuary, the noises grew clearer, solidifying into a scene that would haunt my nights for decades to come. I remember the icy floorboards beneath my small feet, my breath visible in the dim light as I made my way down the hallway. In that unheated space, our father had my mother pinned against the wall, one hand at her throat, the other gripping a knife that caught the weak light from the kitchen.

My oldest brother Gus was the first to move, inserting himself between our parents with a courage I still struggle to comprehend. Butch followed, and suddenly the narrow hallway was filled with shifting shadows as my brothers fought to subdue our father. My arms wrapped around myself for warmth as much as for comfort while I watched the violence unfold. The struggle seemed to last forever, though it was probably only minutes. When it ended, we all retreated to our beds as if this was just another night in the Butler household. In many ways, it was. I burrowed under thin blankets that offered little protection against the cold, my body shivering from both fear and the frigid air.

That night marked the beginning of my complicated relationship with sleep. Even now, nearly forty-eight years later, with a peaceful home of my own and a loving family who has never known such violence, I find myself fighting against the pull of darkness. My wife and sons sleep soundly in our gun-free, knife-free, fire-free home—a home I keep at a steady, comfortable temperature, a small but significant rebellion against my past. Yet I sit awake, still that five-year-old boy listening for footsteps in the hall, feeling phantom chills even in the warmth of my present life. I've broken the cycle for them, kept the violence and the cold from seeping into another generation, but the memories remain etched in my mind with the persistence of my father's mason work—solid, unmovable, permanent.

Reflection

The echoes of childhood violence reach far beyond the moments of impact. While my experience was extreme, every child carries the emotional imprints of their home life into adulthood. No family achieves perfection, but by adhering to basic principles—showing respect, maintaining physical boundaries, choosing words with care, and providing basic comforts like warmth—we can spare our children from carrying the weight of our worst moments through their lives. The scars may never fully heal, but we can stop new ones from forming.

Forgiveness works best when it is forever because a simple glance back, just for a moment, forces unnecessary redundant pain.

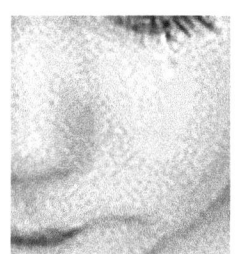

CHAPTER 2

Before the Battles, There Was a War

Walter Butler at his Tavern in East Greenwich circa 1946

To understand the man who became our father, we must step back in time, before the violence and abuse that would later define our childhood. He was, first and foremost, a Navy man - a Gunner's Mate, Third Class who earned one silver and two bronze stars while serving in seven major engagements in the Pacific Theater during World War II. While I cannot excuse his later actions, I believe we must acknowledge the path that led him there.

Born into a family of ten children, our father grew up under the influence of his father Walter, who owned a local bar. This early exposure to alcohol likely shaped his later relationship with drinking. However, it was the tragic events during his military service that truly set the stage for his eventual descent into alcoholism and what we now recognize as post-traumatic stress disorder (PTSD).

The story, as told to our mother, reveals how war's psychological impact transformed him. While serving at sea, he received word that his father had fallen ill. The Navy granted him leave to return stateside, allowing him to be present for his father's final days. The loss devastated him, but there was more hardship to come.

As he prepared to return to duty, his mother fell ill. She pleaded with him not to go back to sea, leaving him with words that would haunt him: "If you go... I will not be here when you return." Torn between his duty to country and family, he chose his military commitment, believing it the honorable path. Six months later, the news he dreaded arrived - his mother had passed away. According to our mother, returning home from war to find both parents gone triggered a depression from which he never fully recovered. His drinking intensified, eventually causing him to miss his reenlistment date and ending his naval career.

I share this history not to defend the violent and abusive actions I witnessed and experienced alongside my siblings and mother. Those acts remain unforgettable and inexcusable. Rather, I feel compelled to acknowledge the man he was before these demons took hold.

Reflection

Through the guidance of my mother, my faith, and my sisters, I've learned that living beyond such pain requires forgiveness. I admit to spending too many years harboring ill will - a natural human response to trauma. Yet the wisdom found in various spiritual traditions - whether Buddha, Catholicism, or Christianity - teaches us that forgiveness can be powerful medicine for a broken heart, a bruised spirit, or emotional damage. The path to healing, I've discovered, lies not in forgetting, but in finding the strength to forgive while honoring our own truth.

"Good friends should be good to you and most certainly must be good for you."

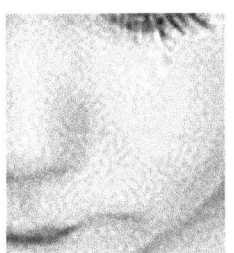

CHAPTER 3

A Sobering Experience

"Ken, you are Woody's brother from another mother," Mrs. Woodward used to say, and forty years later, those words still ring true. In a life shaped by the destructive power of alcoholism, I learned early on that friendship could be either a lifeline or an anchor dragging you down. While my father's "friends" enabled his descent into addiction, my friendship with Dave "Woody"

Woodward showed me a different path.

Woody and I have been inseparable since our teenage years. We shared those quintessential coming-of-age moments together - our first beers, our first motorcycle rides - with the reckless abandon of youth. Now, decades later, we meet weekly for pool, and we still talk about riding motorcycles together, though we laugh about how it'll be at a much more sensible pace and with proper safety gear this time. Our friendship has evolved, but its core remains unchanged. Physical distance never hindered our connection, even when we lived a thousand miles apart. Time hasn't dulled our bond because it's built on something real. The stark contrast between my friendship with Woody and my father's relationships haunts me. While I found a brother figure who helped guide me toward better choices - including helping edit this very book - my father surrounded himself with people who fueled his worst instincts.

The Hope of California

My parents' marriage began crumbling under the weight of alcohol long before I was born. After ten years and seven children, they made a desperate bid for a fresh start. Loading their station wagon with dreams of sobriety and stability, they left Rhode Island for California. It was more than a cross-country trip; it was a pilgrimage toward salvation.

My older sisters speak of California with a wistful tone that suggests what might have been. They describe sun-drenched days free from the dark cloud of alcohol and abuse that had shadowed our family. For fourteen precious months, my mother experienced what normal family life could be. It was during this brief window of peace that I came into the world - baby number eight, born in California during what my mother would later call the happiest months of her married life.

The Return to Rhode Island

But something pulled my father back east. Perhaps it was the familiar haunts, the old friends, the comfortable patterns he'd left behind. Whatever the reason, he packed up our newly expanded family - now with eight kids - and pointed the station wagon back toward Rhode Island. There was no house waiting for us, no job lined up, no real plan beyond return.

Initially, it seemed like things might work out. My father, a skilled mason, established his own company. His reputation for quality brickwork grew, and soon he had men working under him. Money flowed in. But so did the alcohol, enabled by the same "friends" he'd reconnected with. Every Friday night, his week's earnings disappeared into bars across town, leaving nothing for groceries the next day. His success as a mason only made his surrender to alcohol more tragic - a man who could build solid foundations for others couldn't maintain them for his own family.

Reflection

The ripples of alcohol spread far beyond the person drinking, touching every aspect of family life and community. Through my own journey, I've seen how friendships and peer relationships can tip the scales toward either destruction or salvation. The saying "like attracts like" carries profound truth - we become more like those we spend time with, for better or worse.

Forty-five years ago, when my father was struggling, alcoholism lived in the shadows. Families suffered in silence, and resources were scarce. Today's world offers hope through advanced treatment options, support groups, and better understanding of addiction's grip. If someone you love is battling addiction, know that help is available. Professional interventions can work - I've seen them break through walls of denial that seemed impenetrable. The key is reaching out before the foundation crumbles completely.

"Family genes are always part of your DNA, but some values are instilled and some are repelled."

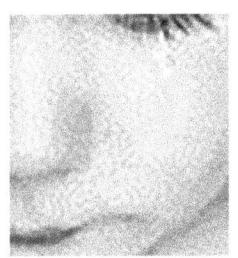

CHAPTER 4

My Genesis

My story is raw and may be upsetting, but it illustrates the universal challenges we all face along the road of life. I share these experiences not just to unburden myself, but to inspire others to acknowledge their own truth. Through my journey, I've learned that humans, regardless of their circumstances, are driven by two fundamental forces: the pursuit of comfort and the avoidance of pain.

I spent forty-six years caught in this exhausting cycle, running from my truth like a fugitive from myself. Each step away from pain only led me deeper into a maze of denial and fear. The irony was that in trying to protect myself, I became my own prison guard, patrolling the borders of what I allowed myself to feel and remember.

Through writing this book, I finally learned to breathe freely in my own skin. Each word written became a key, unlocking chambers of memory I had sealed away. My intention isn't just to share my story, but to demonstrate that while bad things happen to us all, we have the power to reshape our relationship with these experiences. The key lies in creating positive emotional attitudes about any given situation, no matter how challenging it might seem.

Reflection

It has taken me nearly forty-eight years to see my parents as complete human beings – people who existed before giving us life, people with their own struggles and stories. I struggled to accept their choices, fought against their care, but ultimately found peace in forgiveness. This newfound tranquility in my mind is more than just an absence of conflict – it's a presence of understanding that I never thought possible.

The path to this peace wasn't straight or easy. Some days, forgiveness felt like betraying my younger self. Other days, it felt like the only way to set that younger self free. What I've learned is that healing doesn't require us to forget or excuse. Instead, it asks us to understand a profound truth: no matter what the pain, no matter what the sorrow, no matter what the offense, forgiveness isn't about freeing others from responsibility – it's about freeing ourselves from the weight of carrying that pain forward.

In sharing this part of my journey, I hope to illuminate the path for others who might be standing where I once stood, believing that their past defines their future. Your story, like mine, is still being written. The next chapter begins with the choice to face your truth, not as a fugitive, but as someone ready to come home to themselves.

"Some say practice is the mother of mastery. I say, preparation comes way before practice and mastery is best obtained with all of the right tools but if you don't have the tools, go with what you got and enjoy the ride.

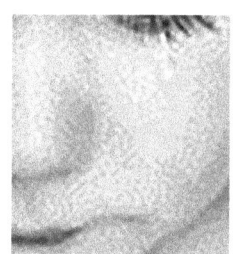

CHAPTER 5

Making Something from Nothing

The morning air bit with early chill as I climbed into my father's pickup truck. I was six years old, and this trash run felt like a sacred ritual – my siblings had made such a fuss about it being my turn to go with Dad. The privilege of riding shotgun wasn't lost on me, even if our destination was just the local dump.

As Dad unloaded our trash, something caught my eye: a discarded bicycle lying among the refuse. Our eyes met when I asked if I could have it, his fierce gaze holding mine for what felt like eternity. "Yes, go get it," he finally said.

I scrambled onto the heap, my heart racing with possibility as I retrieved my treasure. Loading it into the pickup, Dad asked,

"What color would you like to paint it?" "Red," I answered without hesitation.

"How about green, son?" he countered, a hint of something knowing in his voice.

Before leaving, we stopped at the "dump shack" where the guard sat nursing a morning beer. Dad knew him – they exchanged familiar nods as they shared a drink through the truck window. "Got any more of that leftover green paint?" my father asked.

"Park green," the guard confirmed, handing over half a can of that deep, municipal shade that marked every bench and railing in town.

Back home, Dad handed me a six-inch house paintbrush. "If you want to paint your new bike, here you go." No instructions, no warnings about rust or preparation – just a brush and an opportunity.

I attacked the project with six-year-old determination, lathering that park green over every inch of rusty metal. Pride swelled in my chest as I pedaled down the street on my transformed bike. It wasn't until later that I noticed the paint peeling away in strips, leaving a trail of green tears on the asphalt behind me.

Reflection

That day taught me more than just the futility of painting over rust. I learned that opportunities might be buried in unlikely places – even a garbage heap – if you're brave enough to ask for them. The green bike became my first lesson in making something from nothing.

Being poor shaped my creativity in ways I'm still discovering. When resources are scarce, you learn to see possibility in everything, to make things work with whatever you have on hand. Though my time with my father was brief, that morning at the dump left an indelible mark. Every time I find myself improvising or seeing potential in the discarded, I'm that six- year-old boy again, climbing a mountain of trash to claim his treasure.

The green bike's paint may have peeled away, but its lessons stuck fast, coloring every creative endeavor since. It taught me that transformation often begins with seeing value where others see waste, and that sometimes the most meaningful gifts come wrapped in rust and possibility.

"One discouraging word can last a lifetime; one encouraging word can change a life."

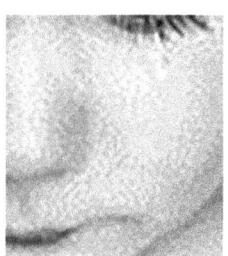

CHAPTER 6

Big Boys Don't Cry

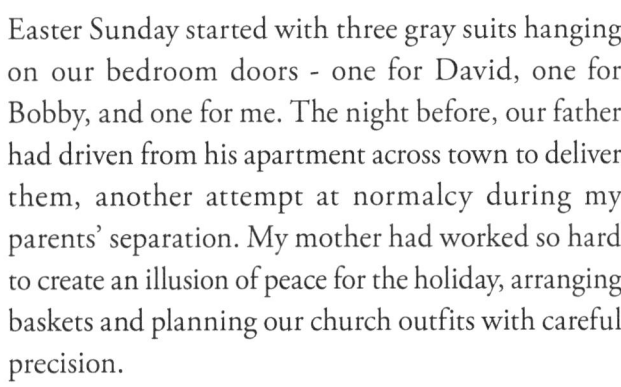

Easter Sunday started with three gray suits hanging on our bedroom doors - one for David, one for Bobby, and one for me. The night before, our father had driven from his apartment across town to deliver them, another attempt at normalcy during my parents' separation. My mother had worked so hard to create an illusion of peace for the holiday, arranging baskets and planning our church outfits with careful precision.

I was headed downstairs when I encountered him on the landing. Maybe I was looking for Mom, or maybe I was just a six-year-old boy wandering his own house. But the stairway suddenly felt like a trap, the shadows from the window stretching long across the worn carpet.

"Big boys don't cry," he taunted, pushing me lightly - not enough to hurt my body, but each shove chipped away at something deeper. The wooden steps creaked beneath my feet as I tried to steady myself. No one came to help. Later, I understood why: in our house, fear had its own gravity, pulling everyone into their own corners, behind closed doors. His presence filled the narrow space, his voice growing sharper with each push. "Don't be a baby," he sneered, the words embedding themselves like splinters in my memory.

Easter morning, I pulled on that gray suit piece by piece, each button and zipper a small victory. In the mirror, I practiced smiling until it looked real. The fabric was stiff and new, uncomfortable in the way fancy clothes always are to little boys, but I wore it like armor. We filed into church, our small procession notably missing its fourth member. The pews were full of perfect Easter Sunday families, but our father's seat remained empty.

After the service, we drove home through streets dappled with spring sunshine. As we turned onto our street, I saw them first - cars, dozens of them, lining both sides of the road. People crowded our front yard, their Easter finest now looking somehow wrong, like costumes at the wrong party. Their faces wore expressions I'd never seen before, a mix of pity and discomfort that made my stomach twist.

"What's the matter?" I asked again and again, but the adults just shook their heads or looked away. Finally, my eight-year-old brother David pulled me aside. His face was pale beneath his Easter suit collar.

"Dad is dead," he said, and then did something I'll never forget. He found a shallow depression in the ground - maybe a dried-up puddle or a dip in the lawn - and thrust his head into it, screaming. The sound that came out of him was primal, raw, like something torn from deep inside. It echoed across our Easter Sunday yard, past the gathered mourners in their pastel dresses and pressed suits, all the way down to wherever lost fathers go.

I wanted to cry then. The tears were there, pressing behind my eyes, filling my throat. But his words from the night before held them back like a dam: "Big boys don't cry." It would be years before I learned how wrong he was, years of holding back tears until I almost forgot how to let them fall.

Reflection

Words have power, especially when spoken to children. They can become the foundation of who we are, or the walls we spend years trying to tear down. If you've said something to a child that you wish you could take back, don't wait. Go to them, apologize, explain why you were wrong. Help them unlearn the lesson before it takes root.

There's an old saying that you can't un-ring a bell, but I've found that's not entirely true. Children understand more than we give them credit for, including genuine remorse and the courage it takes to admit mistakes. Each honest conversation builds a stronger foundation than silence ever could.

Today, I still struggle sometimes to let tears fall freely, but I've found other languages for grief and joy. Through art and writing, I've learned to speak the emotions that once stayed locked inside that little boy in the gray suit. Our father's legacy was one of violence and fear, but it ended with him. When my own children cry, I hold them. When they're afraid, I listen. I'm not a perfect father - no one is - but I've learned that breaking cycles of violence starts with three simple words that my father never said: "I hear you."

"It is often pondered; if we could live our life again what would we do differently? For me, I would be stronger sooner for my siblings."

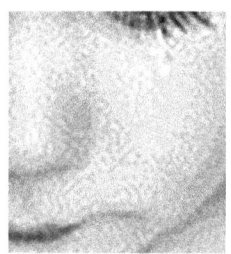

CHAPTER 7

Ashes to Ashes and Dust to Gus

At my father's gravesite was one of only two times I ever saw our mother with her head down. The image is seared into my memory: ten children, a rag-tag bunch, all completely lost. Our father, the breadwinner, was gone. Yet my brother Gus stood there boldly—at twenty-one years old, suddenly the man of the house.

When I was twenty-one, I was driving to Florida with friends to soak up the sun. Gus was taking on the weight of our family. Can you imagine that load on a young man's shoulders? Even now, when my wife leaves on business for just two days, my sons treat me like a substitute teacher. We go from Cheerios for breakfast to SpaghettiOs in record time. The burden my mother carried— raising ten children alone—must have been crushing.

My mother had already weathered the unimaginable: losing her first husband in WWII, and now burying her second. Two husbands lost to war, in one way or another. Yet she never remarried. Years later, when I asked her why, she simply said, "Why would I want another man? I loved your father."

It wasn't until I began writing this book that I realized something devastating: I had never asked what life was like before our father's death. The question hit me like a ton of bricks. I have seven older siblings I could have asked, but perhaps I wasn't ready to hear the answer.

Was our father pure evil? Did he have any redeeming qualities? I gathered the courage to ask my three oldest sisters: "Was there any time, other than our brief period in California, when our home wasn't filled with violence and abuse?"

Their answer was a unanimous "No."

My oldest sister Rosemary's story particularly haunts me. She recalls our father as two different men: brutally mean when drunk, the nicest guy when sober. One winter night in New England, with snow blanketing the ground, their worlds collided. Our father—drunk, not "intoxicated" as we soften it today—was fighting with our mother about his abuse. He kicked her out of the house, and she began walking down the street. Perhaps she was heading to a "friend's" house— though mother later learned this friend had betrayed her, having an affair with our father. He forced Rosemary and our oldest brother out into the snow, underdressed and freezing, to fetch her. When they managed to convince her to return, they all had to knock on their own front door. Our father yanked the children inside, screamed at our mother to get out, and slammed the door in her face. Then he simply sent the kids to bed.

Stories like these repeat throughout our history, but I choose not to dwell there. Instead, I focus on what we became: a great family bound by love and support. The coming chapters will share difficult moments, yes, but more importantly, they'll reveal how I survived and what I did about the awful things that happened.

Reflection

I've always known there were dark stories in our past. Over time,

I built walls through distance and selective memory—an emotional strategy to avoid dealing with pain beyond my own. This self-imposed isolation affected all my relationships. I developed habits like not remembering names, not because I disliked people, but because it kept me from getting close. There's probably a clinical term for this, but for me, it was simple self-preservation against inevitable hurt and broken trust.

Today, my life looks different. I have genuine friendships at all levels—healthy, respectful relationships with people whose names I know and cherish. My family ties are stronger than ever, and writing this book has brought us even closer together. Sometimes, facing the past is the only way to truly embrace the future.

*"When life hands you nothing,
not even lemons, then you must start a water
stand and then build from there.*

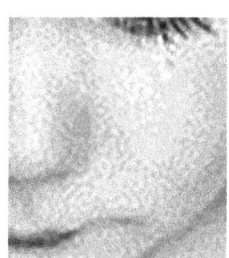

CHAPTER 8

Poor Kenny

Being "poor" is a state of mind. My state of poorness led to creativity and prosperity - if you're willing to look and willing to try, opportunity exists everywhere, even in the depths of poverty.

In the early 1950s, my father's masonry business thrived, with fifteen to twenty men working under him. But alcoholism changed everything. Our family's descent from relative comfort to stark poverty shaped my earliest memories and taught me lessons I'd carry throughout my life.

I was the eighth child, and when my father died, the harsh reality of our situation crystallized. I understood, with the strange clarity that sometimes

visits children, that I would largely be on my own going forward. But rather than crushing my spirit, this realization sparked something unexpected: an almost limitless capacity for imagination.

In our house, necessity birthed creativity. My brothers and I transformed our sisters' shoes into sleek racing cars, their heels becoming spoilers and their soles smooth highways. Our older brothers' work boots became mighty construction trucks, their steel toes perfect for pushing through imaginary dirt and debris. We created entire cities from discarded cardboard, our own miniature world where poverty couldn't follow.

I remember one winter when we couldn't afford proper toys for Christmas. Instead of despairing, we spent weeks beforehand collecting bottle caps and creating an elaborate marble- style game, complete with hand-drawn scoring zones and rules we'd invented ourselves. That game provided more hours of entertainment than any store-bought toy could have offered. Through reading and observation, I've come to understand that all living beings seek two fundamental things: comfort and the avoidance of pain. But how we pursue these basic needs varies dramatically across circumstances. One family might seek comfort in a seven-thousand- square-foot home, while another finds it under a bridge. The millionaire works to avoid the pain of losing millions in the stock market, while someone experiencing homelessness fights to avoid the pain of frostbite. The core desire remains the same - it's just the manifestation that differs. For fifty-six years, I worked tirelessly to avoid pain, and only recently began to truly feel comfort. This isn't about financial status - I'm talking about finally feeling at home in my own skin. Like many survivors of domestic violence, my journey had two distinct phases: first surviving, then learning to thrive. The transition didn't happen overnight. It came through years of self-discovery, therapy, and gradually learning to face my past instead of running from it. In my thirties, I finally achieved one of my childhood dreams - purchasing a classic 1974 red Corvette. But my younger brother Robert, always keeping me grounded, gave me a gift that meant far more: a handcrafted car made from an old shoe, reminiscent of our childhood toys. That shoe-car sits in my workshop today, one of my most treasured possessions. Robert's strength has always inspired me - his ability to find good in this world, even in its darkest corners, taught me resilience I couldn't have learned anywhere else.

Reflection

We've all heard the saying about making lemonade when life gives you lemons. But for many of us, even the lemons aren't there to begin with. That's when you must look beyond the tangible and create your dreams from thin air. If you can't make lemonade, maybe you start with an ice- cold water stand. The key is to start somewhere, anywhere, and build from there.

Never give up on dreaming, hoping, and creating something from nothing. I became a master at pretending, and that led me to dream big. Today, my dreams have evolved beyond material success. My wife often tells me, "If you ever make being financially-rich a goal, we'll be set for life because you always complete your goals and reach your dreams." She knows that money doesn't drive me. Instead, my dreams focus on seeing advances in medical research, particularly in finding a cure for Multiple Sclerosis, a cause that has become deeply personal to our family. Don't misunderstand - money can bring certain comforts and solve real problems. But the creativity, resilience, and hope that poverty taught me? Those are riches that can't be measured in dollars and cents.

"Trust no one for mankind has proven its capacity for evil over and over again. Trust not the church or man but trust in your own relationship with your God."

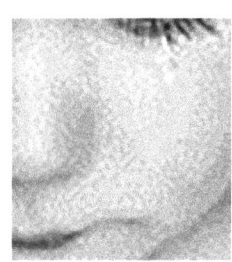

CHAPTER 9

Keeping My Head above Water

I was around six years old when my older brother Butch took us out to the dock on Bellevue Pond. The wooden planks felt warm and rough beneath my bare feet, warmed by the summer sun. The gentle lapping of water against the dock posts created a rhythm that would soon be shattered. Butch had rowed us out there, promising me a special boat ride after he dropped off the other kids. His voice was honey-sweet with deception when he convinced me to step onto the dock so he could talk with some friends who were already there.

The breeze carried the scent of pond water and wet wood as I stood there, fidgeting with excitement about my promised ride. Within just a few minutes, Butch turned to me with a smile that didn't reach his fierce sky-blue eyes.

"Kenny, do you want to learn to swim?"

My stomach tightened at his tone, but I wanted to please him. "Yes," I answered nervously, my voice barely above a whisper.

What happened next is seared into my memory with terrifying clarity. His hands seized me, and suddenly I was airborne. The world spun, and then came the shocking cold of the water enveloping me. I thrashed and struggled, my lungs burning as I choked on pond water. Through the splashing, I could hear Butch laughing.

At first, his friends joined in the laughter, but as my struggles grew more desperate, they began begging him to help me. Their voices seemed to come from far away as I fought to keep my head above water.

"Don't be such a cry baby," Butch called out, the words echoing across the water. Then, with a calculating grin and those piercing blue eyes fixed on me, he added, "If you want to get out of the water, you'll have to get out yourself."

Time seemed to freeze in that moment. The world narrowed to just me, the cold water, and my brother's merciless stare as he watched me struggle. Somehow, driven by pure survival instinct, I managed to drag myself onto that dock. The other kids' faces were horror-struck, unable to comprehend how someone could throw their six-year-old brother – who had never learned to swim – into deep water.

That day taught me something crucial about my brother: he was capable of anything. The incident became just one mark in a long pattern of terror that would continue throughout my teenage years. To this day, the smell of pond water can bring back that moment of betrayal in vivid detail.

Reflections

Abuse manifests in many forms – emotional, physical, violent, and sexual. In my life, I experienced them all, both at home and beyond. Like that day at the pond, each instance of abuse was a moment of struggling to keep my head above water, fighting to survive in an environment where those who should have protected me became my tormentors.

The Power of Open Dialogue

What I've learned through my journey is that abuse thrives in silence. Children rarely come forward directly to report abuse, but they often leave breadcrumbs of truth in everyday conversation. This is why taking time to ask children about their day isn't just casual conversation – it's a vital lifeline.

For example, a child who has experienced abuse at summer camp may not come home and declare, "The camp counselor abused me." However, in an open conversation about their day, they might mention something like, "The counselor took me for a walk alone." These seemingly innocent comments can be crucial warning signs for attentive adults.

Breaking the Cycle of Silence

Trust must be earned when dealing with victims of abuse, regardless of their age. Abusers invest considerable effort in cultivating fear to ensure their victims remain quiet. While it may seem extreme to advocate for constant vigilance with your children, I've witnessed how easily crucial warning signs can be missed by guardians. These overlooked signals can have devastating consequences, sometimes even leading to suicide.

Guilt is nearly always the driving force behind abuse survival. What makes this especially complicated is that most abuse comes from family members or those close to the family. The pressure to keep "family secrets" can be overwhelming, but when these secrets are crimes – especially crimes that violate basic human rights and moral codes – they must be exposed. The weight of family secrets nearly drowned me, just like the pond water that day. But just as I found the strength to pull myself onto that dock, I eventually found the courage to break the silence. This is my contribution to ensuring other children might be spared similar struggles to keep their heads above water.

"Be extremely cautious of the champion of any cause. Think of it like this, a wild bear can be warm and fuzzy to look at and you may even be able to get close, and then all of a sudden you are attacked."

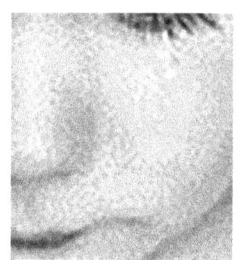

CHAPTER 10

While My Guitar Gently Weeps

The afternoon my sister handed me her boyfriend's old guitar, my fingers couldn't stop tracing the worn wood grain of its body. I was twelve, and in that moment, holding something so precious felt like being trusted with someone else's dreams. "Take good care of it," she said, ruffling my hair. "Maybe you'll be the next Beatles." I promised I would protect it with my life, not knowing how that promise would haunt me.

For those first few weeks, I spent hours in my room, trying to make sense of chord diagrams and fighting through the ache in my fingertips. The guitar became my anchor in a house where supervision was scarce and loneliness was a constant companion. Each tentative strum felt like possibility, like maybe I could build something beautiful out of the silence.

That's when he noticed me. The older kid from down the street, the one everyone seemed to know but nobody really knew. I was practicing on my front steps, fumbling through what I thought might be "Yesterday," when he stopped to listen.

"You're holding it wrong," he said, and somehow those three words created a bridge between us. "I could teach you, if you want."

I remember thinking, How cool is this? I have a friend, finally. When you're twelve and invisible, any attention feels like salvation.

The first lesson seemed legitimate enough. He showed me how to position my fingers, explained things about scales that almost made sense. Then came the suggestion that would change everything: "Why not leave the guitar here so you don't have to carry it home after the lesson?" That seemed okay to me. Reasonable. Adult-like in its practicality.

Then he asked if I wanted to go on an adventure – steal a boat, grab some beer, row out to the cove island, smoke some dope. The way he said it made it sound like an initiation into a secret club, like finally belonging somewhere. I said, "Sure," the word slipping out before I could catch it.

The rest comes in fragments: the gentle lap of water against the boat's hull, the bitter taste of beer, the pills that made everything fuzzy around the edges. What happened next has lived in my bones for forty years, a poison I couldn't purge. He was methodical in his manipulation, using the theft of the boat as leverage, threatening to tell everyone I was queer if I spoke up. The guitar became hostage to my silence.

That silence became a second skin, like wearing a t-shirt that shrinks tighter and tighter with each passing year. You learn to move differently, to hold your breath, to make yourself small. Walking into a room feels like walking into a spotlight, every person a potential witness to your shame. It's easier to retreat, to build walls, to convince yourself that isolation is the same thing as safety.

For decades, I carried two burdens: the weight of what happened and the guilt of my sister's lost guitar. Every time she mentioned it over the years – "Whatever happened to that old guitar?" – I'd mumble something about losing it, each lie adding another layer to that suffocating t-shirt of silence.

Now I understand he was a predator, skilled in the art of grooming, violation, and intimidation. He knew exactly how to select his target, how to build trust, how to ensure silence. The guitar wasn't just an instrument; it was a tool in his arsenal of control.

Looking back, I see that twelve-year-old boy clearly now, desperate for connection, carrying a burden no child should bear. I want to tell him it wasn't his fault, that the shame belongs to the predator, not the prey. But what I can do instead is break the silence.

Yesterday, I finally told my sister the truth about her guitar. Forty years of silence cracked open, and instead of judgment, I found understanding. The tight t-shirt loosened, just a little, letting me breathe in a way I hadn't in decades.

Here's what I've learned: secrets are the soil in which abusers plant their power. Every silent victim becomes unwitting protection for predators who count on that silence to continue their crimes. The jails would overflow if every abuser was held accountable today, but imagine the healing that would begin. If you're carrying this kind of secret, please know you don't have to carry it alone. Go to the police, a counselor, a trusted friend, a community center – anyone who can help bear witness to your truth.

Yes, sometimes the people we trust the most become the ones who hurt us. But there are also people waiting to help, to listen, to believe. Your voice matters. Your story matters. And it's never too late to let your truth be heard.

I may have lost that guitar, but I'm finally finding my voice. And like every note that ever resonated from those strings, it's meant to be heard.

"You can be blessed or cursed with brothers and there is no such thing as automatic brotherly love that takes a lot of work."

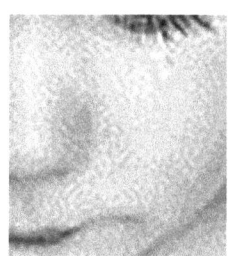

CHAPTER 11

A Wrenching Experience

Growing up in our house meant living with an ever- present undercurrent of tension. My brother Butch ruled our home through fear and unpredictable violence. Every day brought the same question: would this be a peaceful one, or would something – anything – set him off? The pattern started small. He excluded me from family activities – no football, no catch, no ping-pong.

While my other brothers played games and shared laughter, I watched from the sidelines, each exclusion slowly chipping away at my confidence. But it was two specific incidents that transformed my understanding of just how dangerous Butch's violence could become.

I was thirteen when the first incident seared itself into my memory. Butch came home in one of his moods, accusing me of stealing his cigarettes. I hadn't taken them – would never have dared – but the truth didn't matter to him. Something in his eyes told me this wasn't going to be like the usual confrontations. Still, when he called me upstairs to help him with something, I went. Hope died hard in our house, and some part of me still believed that maybe, just maybe, this time would be different.

The wooden stairs creaked under my feet as I climbed. Each step felt heavier than the last as I caught sight of his expression – that look I'd learned to dread. Before I could react, he grabbed me by the neck. In his other hand, he held a wrench, nearly three feet long, its metal cold and unyielding. The next moments exist in my memory with terrible clarity: the rough texture of the window frame, the distant sound of traffic below, the way the winter air bit at my skin as he dangled me out the second-story window. The wrench pressed against my neck, pinning me between the tool and the house. My screams seemed to float away on the wind, losing power with each desperate plea for him to stop. But the more I begged, the harder he pressed, the wrench digging deeper into my flesh.

Inside the house, I knew my mother and siblings were there. I could almost picture them frozen in place, the way we all did when Butch's rage took over. Nobody dared intervene – we'd learned that lesson too many times before. The physical mark around my neck eventually faded, but something else took root that day: a fear of heights that persists even now. Sometimes people chuckle when they learn about it, and I'll make a light joke about holding my wife's purse while she rides the scary rides at Disney. How could they understand that a black belt in martial arts, someone who projects confidence in so many areas of life, still carries that terror? That's the true legacy of domestic violence – the invisible scars that reshape your world.

But the most haunting memory, the one that revealed the full extent of what Butch was capable of, came when he turned his violence toward our mother. It started over something trivial – most of his explosions did. What remains burned in my memory isn't the trigger but the aftermath: our mother on the floor, Butch's casual "Sorry, Mom" as he helped her up, as if he hadn't just shattered another boundary we thought he'd never cross. The look in his eyes in that moment showed us all how far he might go, and that knowledge settled into our bones like winter frost.

For reasons I never understood, Butch focused most of his attention on me. The abuse took many forms, each leaving its own particular scar. But living in that house, knowing that violence could erupt at any moment, even with our mother sitting right there – that was its own kind of torture. We lived in a world where normal family moments could transform into nightmares without warning.

It was martial arts that finally offered me a path forward. When I joined the school, I wasn't looking to become a fighter – I was looking for a way to survive. What I found was something far more valuable than combat skills. Each class built something new inside me, replacing the foundation of fear with something stronger. Martial arts taught me that true strength isn't about dominating others; it's about developing an unshakeable core of self- worth that no one can take away. Through practice and dedication, I discovered a different kind of power – not the destructive force I'd grown up with, but the strength to be better, to do better, to break the cycle of violence.

Reflection

Today, I understand that what happened in our home wasn't just about physical abuse. Abusers like Butch create an atmosphere of terror that seeps into every corner of family life. The violence doesn't need to be physical to leave lasting damage – verbal and emotional abuse can be equally devastating, distorting what children come to see as "normal." This distortion ripples outward, affecting how we build relationships, raise our own children, and move through the world. Looking back, I see how that terrified thirteen-year-old boy began a journey toward becoming someone who could stand against abuse in all its forms. This isn't just my story – it's a window into the reality that too many people live with behind closed doors. Every form of abuse, whether physical, verbal, or emotional, violates basic human rights. These stories need to be told, these crimes brought to light, so that others might recognize their own power to break free and heal.

The scars remain – some visible, others hidden – but they no longer define who I am. They're reminders of where I've been and why I choose, every day, to be something different than what I witnessed.

Through martial arts, therapy, and years of internal work, I've learned that while we can't change our past, we can change its power over our future. That frightened boy at the window became a man determined to help others find their own path to strength.

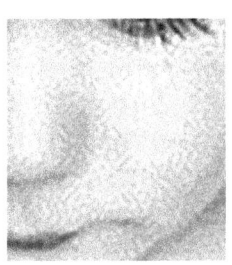

"Big brothers are put on earth to protect younger brothers.

Hey, Big Brother

My brother Gus stepped into our father's shoes when I was just a kid, shouldering the weight of our family patriarch far too young. Looking back, I see how that responsibility shaped him – a teenager forced to become a man overnight, helping raise his younger siblings while navigating his own grief.

I was thirteen when my life changed course. After our father's death, our family had scattered like leaves in the wind. I ended up in Florida with my older sister, though the circumstances that led me there have blurred with time. Maybe it was my mother's struggle to keep us all together, or maybe it was just the chaos that follows loss. Whatever the reason, I found myself adrift, angry, and looking for trouble. When I got in trouble hanging out with the wrong kid, silly stuff, nothing too dangerous but enough that stealing a bike, the judge gave me two options: reform school or living with my brother Gus. I thought I'd hit the jackpot – my cool older brother would surely be better than some juvenile detention center.

I couldn't have been more wrong about it being an easy ride. When

Gus picked me up from the airport, his stern face told me everything I needed to know. The bright smile I'd worn faded as he lectured me the entire drive home. This wasn't going to be the fun escape I'd imagined. Gus and his wife Brenda lived in a modest house with their young son, my nephew. From day one, Gus made it clear that this was my chance to turn things around, and he wasn't going to let me waste it. Every morning started at 5:30 AM – no exceptions. He taught me how to make my bed with military precision, how to iron my clothes, and how to carry myself with dignity. "A man takes care of himself," he'd say, showing me how to shave, even though I barely had peach fuzz. When I slouched, he'd tap my shoulder.

When I mumbled, he'd make me repeat myself clearly.

The structure I'd been missing slowly rebuilt me. Brenda's quiet strength provided a different kind of support – she made sure I had proper meals, helped with my homework, and gave me the first taste of what a stable home felt like. Their house smelled like coffee in the morning and whatever Brenda was cooking for dinner in the evening. It was the first place I remember feeling truly safe. I fought against their rules at first, but Gus never raised a hand to me – he didn't need to. His disappointment was punishment enough. Instead, he channeled my angry energy into wrestling. "You want to fight something?" he'd said. "Fight on the mat." I joined the team, and for the first time in my life, I found something I was good at. My undefeated record became a source of pride, not just for me but for Gus too. I can still see him in the stands at matches, nodding with approval when I'd win.

The turning point came before my first school dance. I had nothing to wear and was ready to skip it, but Gus wouldn't hear of it. He opened his closet and pulled out his best clothes – pressed slacks, a crisp button-down shirt, and a tie he taught me to knot properly. Standing in front of the mirror, dressed in my brother's clothes, I saw myself differently. I wasn't just some troubled kid anymore. I looked like somebody's son, somebody's brother, somebody who mattered.

Years later, my wife and I took in Gus's son when he needed a place to stay. It felt like completing a circle, passing on the stability that Gus and Brenda had given me. We broke the cycle of abuse that had haunted our family, but some cycles are harder to break. Gus died alone in his home, found by his son. The details of his death remain unclear, but the tragedy of it haunts me. The man who had been there for so many died with no one by his side.

Sometimes I wonder if I could have done more in his final years. After getting my life together, I'd moved away, thinking distance from my past would help heal old wounds. I was wrong. In trying to escape the painful parts of my history, I'd also distanced myself from the good parts – from the brother who had saved me.

Looking up at the stars some nights, I talk to him. I tell him about the man I've become, the family I've built, the lives I've touched. All of it started with him, with those months under his roof when he refused to give up on me. He stood up as a young man when our father died, carried burdens no teenager should have to bear, and somehow found the strength to not just survive but to help others.

You deserve to rest in peace, big brother. I hope you know that your love and care echo through generations now. Every time I help someone who's struggling, every time I choose patience over anger, I'm passing on what you taught me. That's your legacy, Gus, and it lives on.

Reflection

Family is rarely all good or all bad – it exists in shades of gray. In my effort to escape painful memories, I made the mistake of distancing myself from everyone, including those who had shown me love and support. I learned too late that you can maintain boundaries with toxic family members without cutting off those who lift you up. Gus taught me that family isn't just about blood – it's about who shows up for you, who builds you up, who helps you become better. Don't let the hurt caused by some blind you to the love offered by others. Embrace those who embrace you, and never let anyone's darkness dim the light others bring to your life.

The Lost Chapter

After leaving Gus's house, my memories dissolve into darkness. This is the hardest part of my life to write about, because from age thirteen to sixteen, I simply can't place myself anywhere. Those years exist as a vortex of time in my life - a swirling, empty space where memories should be. The gaps in my recollection are both frustrating and frightening. Sometimes I lie awake at night, trying to piece together where I was, who I was with, but the memories remain just out of reach.

What I do know is that during this period, I found myself once again with nowhere to stay. No home, no stability, no safe harbor. Somehow, inexplicably, I ended up living with Butch. It sounds crazy, I know. Looking back now, I still can't understand how or why I landed there.

But that situation turned out to be more chaotic than anything I had experienced before.

"Family equals people you trust. Relatives equal people in your life through marriages and relationships that are not always in line with your values. The skill is to identify the difference and make a stand."

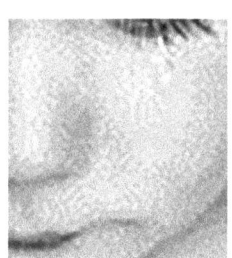

CHAPTER 13

An Ax to Grind

My older brother Butch offered me a place to stay in the winter of 1982 when I lost my car detailing job at a local dealership. I'd always feared him as a kid, even though the history of abuse was still fresh, I was willing to risk because I had nowhere else to go. Desperate is the word. The age gap meant we weren't particularly close. His house wasn't much - a small rancher on the outskirts of town - but I was grateful for any roof over my head. The unemployment checks barely covered my contribution to his household, but he seemed satisfied with the arrangement and the free labor I provided.

Growing up, we'd all seen our father brandish his ax when he was angry. The sound of it hitting wood became the soundtrack of our childhood, along with mother's hushed warnings to stay quiet, stay still, stay out of his way. Maybe that's why the familiar wooden handle of Butch's ax made me uneasy every time I passed it in the garage. I told myself he just used it for firewood, like any normal person would.

One morning in early spring, I was cleaning the living room - "earning my keep" as Butch liked to remind me. The windows were open, letting in the first warm breeze of the season. That's when I heard it: the scrape of a chair against linoleum, followed by a scream that made my blood run cold.

The scene in the kitchen stopped my heart. Butch had his wife cornered by the refrigerator, the ax raised high above his head. Everything slowed down like a nightmare. I saw the morning sun glinting off the blade, the terror in her eyes, the way her fingers splayed against the yellow wallpaper behind her. She dove to the side just as the ax came down, the blade embedding itself deep in the linoleum floor with a sound that echoed through my bones.

The thunk of metal hitting floor broke something in me. While Butch wrestled with the stuck ax, cursing and growing more enraged by the second, I backed away silently. His wife's eyes met mine for just a moment - the same look I'd seen in my mother's eyes a hundred times before. I went to my room, packed my few belongings in a duffel bag, and walked out the front door. I never said a word about what I'd seen - not to my mother, not to my siblings, not to anyone. My silence felt like protection at the time - for his wife, for our family name, for my own peace of mind. But every year of silence was another year his wife lived in danger, another year the cycle continued.

Over the decades that followed, I often thought about that morning in Butch's kitchen. Every time I heard about domestic violence on the news, I'd see that ax swinging through the air. I'd wonder if I should have done more, said more, been braver. The weight of that silence grew heavier with each passing year.

Thirty-five years later, I learned that Butch had also been a victim of our father's violence. The revelation hit me hard but didn't surprise me. The sins of the father had become the sins of the son, passed down like a dark inheritance. The scope and intensity of what Butch endured as a child, I won't detail here. Some wounds are better left unnamed.

When Butch was dying of cancer in 2018, we finally talked about that spring morning. His hands, once strong enough to swing an ax, were thin and trembling as he spoke of his regrets. His remorse seemed genuine, but some actions leave marks that even forgiveness can't erase. I made my peace with him as best I could. God have mercy on his soul.

Reflection

The hardest truth about abuse is how it spreads through families like poison through a bloodline. Statistics show most abuse begins at home, which creates a suffocating barrier to getting help. Who do you tell when the people who should protect you are the ones causing harm? I learned too late that my silence, though born of fear and family loyalty, only protected the abuser. If you're in an abusive situation - whether it's psychological, physical, sexual, or emotional - you must understand that no one has the right to hurt you. Age and fear often conspire to keep victims quiet, but silence is a room without doors. You must be strong enough to speak, to run, to seek help. I've seen enough to know that any decent person or family will help if you just ask.

The pattern of abuse feeds on fear and silence. The only way to break it is to find your voice.

"Hard work pays off and it shows."

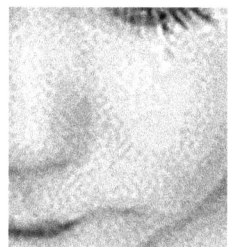

CHAPTER 14

Hard Work Pays Off
School of Hard knocks

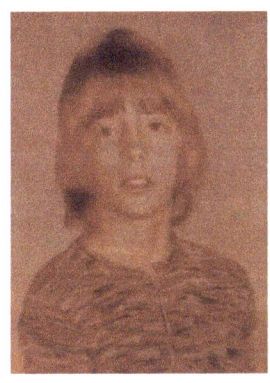

As one of the youngest of ten children, I learned early that independence wasn't just a choice – it was a necessity. The photograph on my mother's dresser shows a young boy with a tentative smile, but what it doesn't c apture is the weight of circumstances already shaping my understanding o f survival and self- reliance. Behind that smile lay years of domestic violence, emotional distress, and various forms of abuse that no child should endure. These experiences, though devastating, planted the seeds of a determination that would later define not only my approach to life but also my journey as a parent.

By thirteen, I understood the harsh mathematics of our family economics. My mother's social security support would diminish as each child turned eighteen, creating an unofficial countdown to independence. In our small military town of North Kingstown, RI, the path forward seemed predetermined – most people ended up at Electric Boat, the shipyard that promised good money for backbreaking work.

But even as a teenager, I knew I wanted something different, even if I couldn't yet define what that "something" was.

The decision to quit high school came from a place of practical necessity rather than rebellion. I threw myself into whatever work I could find – dishwasher, gas station attendant, landscaper, factory worker. Each job taught me something, but more importantly, each paycheck brought me closer to what I saw as freedom. When I finally saved $500 to buy my first car, a 1966 AMC Rambler Convertible (affectionately known as "Almost a Car" by those familiar with American Motor Company), I thought I'd achieved that freedom. Reality, however, had other plans.

The car failed inspection, needing $1,200 in repairs – more than twice what I'd paid for it. For eight months, that symbol of independence sat immobile in my sister's driveway, a daily reminder of the gap between dreams and reality. Despite having seven older siblings, no offers of help came. At the time, this felt like confirmation of my solitude, reinforcing my belief that I had to make it entirely on my own. Looking back now, I understand that most of my siblings were fighting their own battles for survival, unable to extend the help I so desperately wanted.

Those months of watching my car sit idle could have broken my spirit. Instead, they hardened my resolve. I worked extra shifts, saved every dollar, and eventually earned enough to make the repairs. The day I finally drove that convertible, top down and running smooth, I felt a pride that no handed-down vehicle could have given me. That car became more than transportation – it was proof that determination could bridge the gap between wanting and having.

Years later, as a father to my sons EJ and TY, I found myself wrestling with how to pass on the value of hard work without transferring the pain that taught me its importance. A conversation with my nephew Aubrey challenged my thinking. "Do you think that is necessary?" he asked when I explained my philosophy about making my kids work for everything. "Why make your kids struggle like we did?"

His questions forced me to confront an uncomfortable truth: in my determination to teach self- reliance, I risked recreating the very isolation I had experienced. The answer, I realized, lay in finding balance – teaching the value of hard work while providing the guidance I never had. This philosophy was put to the test during a simple fence-painting project in 2009. I assigned both boys equal sections of fence, giving each the same supplies and offering $1 per post painted. TY took the left side, EJ the right. When EJ ran out of paint and asked for more, I provided it without comment. Once finished, I paid TY $8 for his eight posts but gave EJ only $6 for the same number. The confusion on EJ's face prompted an important lesson about resource management and the ound hidden costs of work.

The following week, when we painted the inside of the fence, EJ approached the task differently. He worked carefully, managed his supplies, took and completed the job efficiently.

Today, as a young adult, EJ consistently receives praise from employers for his work ethic. But what makes me proudest isn't just that he works hard – it's that he understands why he's working and how to work smart.

My journey from a trauma-scarred child to a parent teaching life lessons through fence painting represents more than just personal growth. It's about learning that while hard work is essential, it doesn't have to be solitary. True strength lies not just in being able to do everything alone, but in knowing how to work through challenges while accepting guidance and support. This is the legacy I hope to leave my children – not just the ability to survive on their own, but the wisdom to thrive with others.

"Influences around you don't always have to influence you in a negative way. A little bad company can push you in the right direction."

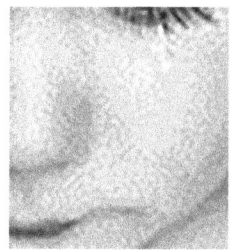

CHAPTER 15

FLORIDA
or BUST!

The summer heat rippled off the asphalt as I stared at my friend's 1972 Monte Carlo. Everything I owned hung from a rack of clothes in the back seat, along with what little cash I'd managed to scrape together. Florida represented something I desperately needed: escape, a fresh start, maybe even hope. After everything that had happened back home, anywhere else had to be better. "You ready?" my friend Frank asked, jangling his keys. I'd known him for six months – not long, but long enough for him to offer me a way out when I needed one most. He'd made arrangements for us in advance, called some people he knew down in Palm Beach County. At the time, I was grateful for any plan that pointed forward.

The drive south felt like crossing into another world. The familiar streets of home faded into endless highways, palm trees, and a humidity that clung to my skin like a second layer of worry. We pulled up to a small house just as the sun was setting. A guy with a deep tan and a knowing smile met us at the door.

"Welcome to sunny Florida," he drawled, "where a lot of shady people hang out." I forced a laugh, but something in his tone should have warned me. I was twenty-one, naive, and completely unprepared for what that casual warning really meant.

The struggle started immediately. Weeks passed, and every job application led to nothing. The guys we were staying with kept odd hours, had mysterious visitors, and spoke in coded phrases I pretended not to hear. I'd lie awake at night on my borrowed bed, listening to hushed conversations and trying to convince myself I was imagining things. Later, I'd learn that cocaine and marijuana had been stored right under that same bed – a fact that still sends chills through me when I think about how close I came to being caught up in something I couldn't escape. After months of searching, I finally landed a job at TGI Fridays. For the first time since arriving in Florida, I felt like I could breathe. The work was steady, the tips were decent, and I managed to save enough to buy a used truck. I found my rhythm in the restaurant's controlled chaos, learning the menu front to back, taking pride in remembering regular customers' orders before they spoke.

But just as things began to stabilize, Frank announced he was moving to a better place – one I couldn't afford. Our paths had been diverging for weeks, his income somehow growing faster than seemed possible from his vague "business opportunities." I couldn't follow, and suddenly found myself living with another group of strangers, forced to leave TGI Fridays because the commute was impossible without reliable transportation.

The family I stayed with owned a gas station, and that's where I landed – a high school dropout pumping gas under the merciless Florida sun. But even then, I refused to let go of hope. I memorized regular customers' preferences, learned every car's quirks, and made that concrete island between the pumps my stage for proving I could excel at anything, even if it wasn't where I wanted to be.

"You're the best attendant we've ever had," customers would say, and I'd hold onto those words like lifelines. I knew – knew in my bones – that I could do more if the right opportunity appeared.

Then came the night one of my roommates took my car without asking and crashed it. He had settlement money from a lawsuit and handed me $1,500 in cash for repairs. The car was still drivable, and my job was walking distance. For the first time in months, I felt a window of opportunity cracking open. That's always been my nature – finding the silver lining, the hidden chance in every setback.

The next morning, the money was gone. Every single dollar. The uncle who owned the house turned cold when I confronted him about it, and within hours, I found myself on the street. No job, no real home, no car, and no money. Rock bottom had a Florida address, and I was living there.

Then I remembered the martial arts contract I'd signed just days before – $23 a month at a local Tae Kwon Do school. It felt ridiculous now, that commitment to something so far from basic survival. I walked to the school, ready to beg out of the contract, my last shred of dignity crumbling.

Instead of the sales person, Master Kim stepped in to meet with me. He was shorter than me but carried himself with an authority that filled the room. His eyes seemed to look straight through my excuses to something I couldn't yet see in myself.

"If you quit this," he said, his accent thick but his words precise, "you will quit everything in your life."

The truth of it hit me like a physical blow. "How can I pay for this?" I gestured at myself – unemployed, homeless, broken. "I don't have a job, a place to live, I have nothing."

Master Kim's expression didn't change. "You have yourself," he said, "and you can begin training tomorrow." He reached into his pocket and pulled out a ten-dollar bill. "Go get a haircut, come back, and you will have a place to stay, weekly pay, and a positive future." That moment transformed everything. The next day, I began what they called "training" – ten- hour shifts, six days a week. I moved into a house with four other trainees, all of us working toward our second-degree black belts and the chance to teach Tae Kwon Do at my own school. We were a strange sort of family, bound together by shared discipline and dreams.

The days blurred into a rhythm of physical and mental challenges. Every muscle ached, but my mind grew sharper. I learned forms and techniques, but more importantly, I learned focus, dedication, and the art of pushing past perceived limits. My body transformed, hardening into a tool I could trust, even as my spirit began to heal.

"Instructor Butler," Master Kim would say, watching me move through complex forms, "physically you are the most talented martial artist I have ever seen. However," and here he would always pause, making sure I understood the weight of his words, "you must also master your emotions."

I didn't know then how crucial that lesson would become. I was in the best shape of my life, both physically and mentally, but life was about to test everything Master Kim had taught me in ways I never could have imagined.

Looking back, I understand now what he meant about mastering emotions. The skills I learned on those training mats – patience, discipline, the ability to face fear and pain without breaking – they were preparing me for challenges far beyond the dojang. Every drop of sweat was building not just a better fighter, but a stronger person. And I would need every ounce of that strength for what waited just around the corner.

"Circumstances can open doors but you must walk through."

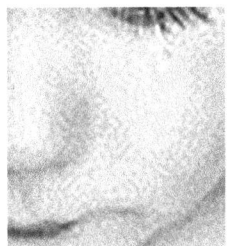

CHAPTER 16

Work, Train, Eat, Sleep

The sweat dripped onto the polished wooden floor of Master Kim's martial arts school as I demonstrated a complex form for my evening class. Three years ago, I had been pumping gas with no direction. Now, I stood as a senior instructor, teaching youth and family classes with a profound sense of purpose. The transformation hadn't been easy, but Master Kim had seen something in me that I hadn't yet recognized in myself.

When Master Kim awarded me a scholarship, I almost laughed. A scholarship? I didn't even have a high school diploma. But that moment sparked something inside me – a realization that I could be more than my past suggested. With the $600 award, I hired Chris Wagner, a fellow student and county jail GED instructor, to prepare me for the test. Each night after training until 10:00 PM, Chris and I would walk home together, my muscles aching from training and my mind stretching to grasp concepts I'd missed years ago. The basics that every person needs that I could not get at the time.

Starting at an eighth-grade level wasn't easy, but it ignited an excitement I'd never felt about education before. For three months, we worked tirelessly. The day my diploma arrived, I was alone – fitting for someone who had grown accustomed to facing life's biggest moments in solitude. My tutor's words echoed in my mind: "If the envelope is regular size, it's bad news. If it's flat and big, it's great news." When I saw that large envelope, my hands trembled. Among all my achievements – the awards, citations, certificates, and eventually a degree – that high school diploma remains my proudest accomplishment, hanging with honor in my studio. I could not have been prouder of myself. Master Kim even put me in one of his books. Master Kim gave me the opportunities to be a much better person. And it never hurts to have the skills to protect yourself.

With one year left in my training before I could open my school, I had crystallized five major goals:

Earn my high school diploma Achieve my second-degree black belt Graduate from the martial arts academy Save $5,000

Open my own school

The path seemed clear, each goal building upon the last. But life had other plans.

The Diagnosis

It started during my physical examination before testing for my second-degree black belt. "There's a lump on your right testicle," the physician said matter-of-factly. "We'll need to do a biopsy. Come back in four hours for the results." He paused, his expression growing serious. "If I were a betting man, I'd say you have cancer. We just need to determine if the tumor is malignant."

Those four hours defined me. I walked to Lake Eola, finding a bench where I could sit alone with my thoughts. The Florida sun beat down, but I barely noticed. Being alone wasn't new to me – I'd never consider calling my mother to say, "I might have cancer. I'll call you back in a few hours." On that bench, watching the lake's surface ripple in the afternoon light, I made a promise to myself: if I lived, I would never take another day for granted.

At 4:00 PM on August 29, wearing my tan Tae Kwon Do shirt, black sweat pants, and white sneakers, I heard those three words that would change everything: "You have cancer."

Round One: The Initial Battle

Walking into the martial arts school that evening felt surreal. A student was there, working on a newsletter article about my life story leading up to graduation. She snapped a photo as I entered – little did she know her story was about to take a dramatic turn.

The first surgery was scheduled for the very next day. But even as I faced this diagnosis, my focus remained fixed on graduation. When the physician said, "Mr. Butler, I want to bring you up on current affairs… You have stage three cancer and we need to operate now," my response surprised even me.

"No, Sir. I must graduate."

The inner turmoil was intense – battling between my driving goal and the urgent need to save my life. But the thought of getting through everything I had endured and not achieving my goal seemed unbearable. The martial arts had taught me about fighting spirit; now it was time to prove it.

Round Two: Testing Mind and Body

Two weeks after the first surgery, still recovering but determined, I tested for my second- degree black belt and all the credentials needed to open my own school. The physical demands were extraordinary, but the mental challenge was even greater. Every kick, every form, every sparring match was a declaration: cancer would not deny me this achievement.

Round Three: The Major Surgery

The Radical Node Dissection came next – a procedure that felt as invasive as its name suggested. They made an incision from my groin to my chest, removed all internal organs temporarily, and extracted positive lymph nodes. When I opened my eyes after five hours of surgery and three hours of recovery, my mother, brother Gus, and nephew Joe were by my bedside. In that moment, Master Kim's teachings about family, both blood and chosen, resonated deeply.

Round Four: The Chemical Warfare

Chemotherapy began four weeks after the second surgery. Cisplatin became my new opponent – a powerful but brutal ally in this fight. The side effects were relentless: nausea, fatigue, peripheral neuropathy, loss of appetite. My body changed dramatically, documented in photographs that showed my transformation from a strong martial artist to a gaunt fighter of a different kind.

The martial arts had taught me about endurance, about pushing through pain, about maintaining mental strength when the body wants to quit. During treatment, these lessons took on new meaning. Sometimes I would cry during practice, my tears mixing with sweat as I pushed through forms and techniques. The physical discipline of Tae Kwon Do became my anchor to normality, my way of proving I was still me.

Round Five: Reclaiming Life

The progression of photos tells the story: from July 1986, before diagnosis, through the brutal months of treatment, and into early 1987. Each image marks a milestone: the last day of treatment, two weeks after chemotherapy when it was time to feel again, one month later when healing began in earnest, and finally, March 1987, when I truly began to deal with everything that had happened.

Through it all, the lessons from both martial arts and my history of surviving abuse served me well. Cancer was just another predator, and I had learned long ago how to fight back. The discipline, focus, and indomitable spirit that Master Kim had nurtured in me became my greatest weapons in this battle.

Today, when I teach at my own school, I share not just martial arts techniques but the deeper lessons about perseverance, courage, and the warrior spirit. Every class is a reminder of that promise I made on the bench at Lake Eola – to never take a single day for granted.

1985 A.T.F. SCHOLARSHIP RESULTS ARE IN!

Another Trainee Instructor, Mr. Ken Butler also received an A.T.F. Scholarship Award earlier and has since proudly completed his secondary education earning his G.E.D. through the support and motivation of the American TaeKwon-Do Federation.

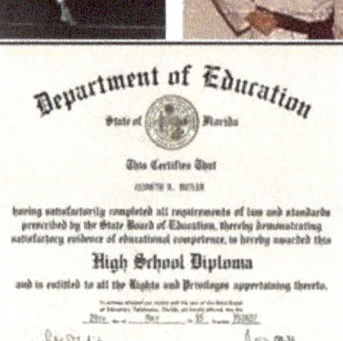

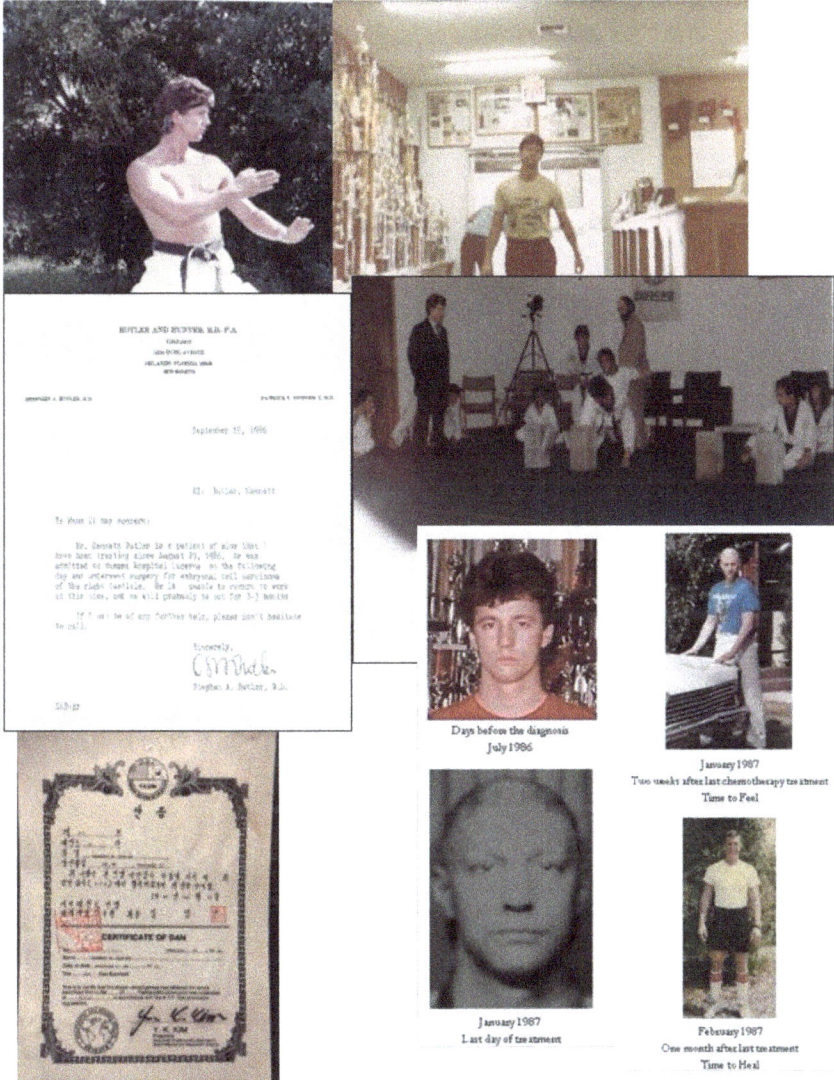

Days before the diagnosis
July 1986

January 1987
Two weeks after last chemotherapy treatment
Time to Feel

January 1987
Last day of treatment

February 1987
One month after last treatment
Time to Heal

CHAPTER 17

Zen with Ken

In the darkest moments of our lives, light often finds unexpected ways to reach us. During the twelve months following my cancer diagnosis, I experienced something profound - a spiritual awakening that transformed my battle into something greater than myself. Through two surgeries and countless hours of chemotherapy, I found myself touched by what I can only describe as divine inspiration. Words would come to me, not as mere thoughts, but as gifts from above, each poem arriving precisely when I needed its message most. Before I share these works, I should mention two miracles that emerged from this valley: I met

Beth, the nurse who would become

my wife, and I discovered my path back to education through art. Sometimes our greatest trials lead us to our greatest blessings. But first, let me take you through the journey that brought me there.

The Beginning: Faith in the Storm

I am Ready, Lord
Written the night before my first surgery

Oh my God hear my cry, please take my soul if
I should die. If it is your will that my body perish or remain,
my trust in thee is the same.

This first poem came to me in the quiet hours when fear threatens to
overwhelm hope. Its simplicity reflected my core belief - that surrender
to something greater than ourselves often becomes our greatest strength.

The Treatment Journey

The First Day of Chemotherapy
When everything felt impossible

The first treatment will start only with the Lord.
Without Him, we could not afford to be as strong.
He will make it quick and short instead of painful and long.
Cancer is on the inside but so is our Lord.
We must always remember he is with us on each accord.
Remember that he loves us; remember we need him.
He will lead us to the father in the sky.
Remember never ask him why.
Only to the Lord, we could never lie.

The Second Day of Chemotherapy
Learning to embrace grace

Lord, I believe you see the physical and mental pain that is ahead for me.
Please give me the wisdom that my sickness is like the transient rain.
Please give me humbleness not to be vain.
Let my faith grow to the highest high.
Help me seek the kingdom in the sky.

Teach me never to ask why.
Open your heart to sing your song, always, always be strong.

The Inner Battle

Alone
Written during a sleepless night in the hospital

I am alone it seems like all the time not only
my body but in my mind. Why must I
always look for something to do or
someone to talk to?
This I have always wondered, how about you?
In these moments of solitude, I began to understand that loneliness
itself could become a teacher. It was during these quiet times that I
first noticed Beth's gentle presence, though neither of us knew then
where our path would lead.

The Pain
On learning to accept what we cannot change

The pain is like the rain, only God controls it,
Some men fear it, some men try to escape it,
some men take it, and aimless men walk in it,
Foolish men play in it but this man deals with it.

Community and Connection

Friends in the Cancer Jail
Dedicated to my fellow warriors in Ward B

Yes, my friends, be strong.
Like your stay, our life is not very long. So if you're down,
remove the frown, and dream of the day when you exchange our
cross for our crown.
This, you carry your whole lifelong. Sometimes

our crosses are filled with sorrow and sometimes
our crosses are filled with songs. So with all your
heart thank God for today and pray your heart
will not be chilled. This may mean a little or this
may mean a lot, but the cross my friend is the
best thing we've got.
So carry it proud whether you're stuck in the cancer jail or getting out.
Jesus did for us, is not that what our life is all about?
So never leave the word, sing, scream, and shout, let
all men know what your life is about.

I wrote this poem after meeting James, Maria, and Robert - fellow patients who taught me that even in our darkest hours, we could lift each other up. Their courage became my courage, their strength my strength. Some of them are no longer with us, but their spirit lives on in these words.

Contemplating Mortality

The Finish
Reflecting on life's temporary nature

Life is like a vapor and death is just one part of human nature.
When no one is sure, how is the same and why is
easy, so we can go on to a better place.
This is called the human race.
After you start and where you finish is all predetermined, and
what direction you run, toward the darkness or toward the sun.
The Next Procedure
Understanding humility People
are such as a blade of grass if
they grow to a boastful size they
will be cut down in a flash.
However, the roots remain and the next procedure is the
same. So try to grow on the inside, not out and not up but stay

low on the out and high on the in so the next procedure will never begin.

Living in the Present

Imagine
Learning to appreciate each moment

Just what would we do if we only had thirty minutes to live.
What you would do first is normally what we would
do last in our everyday life.
So do the things that you would normally save for last
and do them today.
Imagine every day is your last day but is also your very best day.
What If
On earthly attachments

Things of the earth are heavy and hard.
Just what would we do if it sank beneath the
tar? Yes, all things like the tree and the flower,
yes, my friend even the hour.
Yes, we would all cry, surely we would all cry
to the heavens and the sky.
Oh my God, please take me I'm sure men would say but
the men who are heard will be the men who pray.

The Journey's End

The Last Day of Chemotherapy
A revelation of life's purpose

My life is a gift and that gift is encouraged through the human spirit.
That is the thing that will carry me all the days God has given me.
I have only one thing to share with the world and that one thing
is my life.
Finally, I'm not alone and if and when I am alone I will
embrace it with all my heart because it is that place where

I learned so much about living. Imagine that in learning about dying I have learned more about living.

Remorse Not
A final reflection on survival and purpose

The woods are dark yet they inspire hope
The woods are bright yet they can steal the light
The woods are full yet they are not crowded
The woods are cold yet they are full of warmth
The woods are lonely yet they are full of good company.

Remorse not we that made it out of the woods
The reason we made it out is not for us to question.
However, that we have made it out of the woods,
we must help those who are still in the woods
We must help those who are just entering the woods
We must help those who have to go back to the woods
Most of all, we must remember our friends that never
had the chance to walk in the woods.

A New Beginning
After completing my treatment, I knew life would never be the same
- and perhaps that was the greatest blessing of all. With Beth by my
side and a renewed sense of purpose, I made the decision to pursue
my GED and follow my passion for art at college in Ft. Lauderdale.
While working full-time at a warehouse, I attended classes, driven by
the understanding that life's greatest gifts often come disguised as its
greatest challenges.

Beth and I built our life together in Orlando, far from family, learning
to rely on each other completely. In those early days of working and
studying, we discovered that survival isn't just about making it through
the storm - it's about learning to dance in the rain. Through every
challenge, these poems remained our touchstones, reminders of the

grace that carried us through the darkest woods and into the light of a new day.

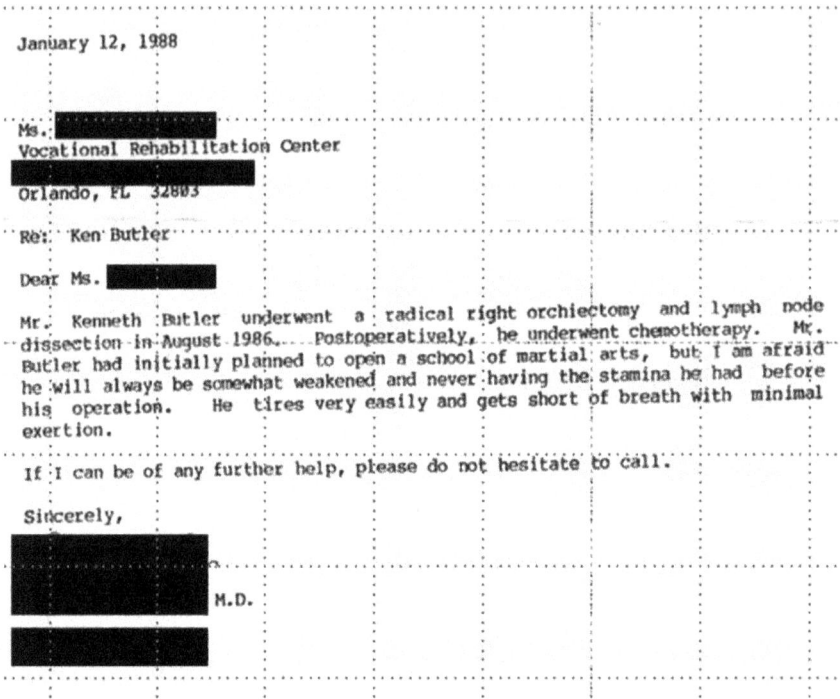

January 12, 1988

Ms. ██████████████
Vocational Rehabilitation Center

Orlando, FL 32803

Re: Ken Butler

Dear Ms. ████████

Mr. Kenneth Butler underwent a radical right orchiectomy and lymph node dissection in August 1986. Postoperatively, he underwent chemotherapy. Mr. Butler had initially planned to open a school of martial arts, but I am afraid he will always be somewhat weakened and never having the stamina he had before his operation. He tires very easily and gets short of breath with minimal exertion.

If I can be of any further help, please do not hesitate to call.

Sincerely,

██████████████

██████████████ M.D.

██████████████

CHAPTER 18

Our Love Story

The white walls of my Central Florida apartment seemed to close in on me that morning as I stared at my reflection. My hands trembled as I tried to button my shirt, the simple task made monumental by the chemotherapy coursing through my system. I had thought I could do this alone – fight cancer on my own terms in my own space. But as I slumped against the bathroom counter, unable to even drive myself to treatment, I realized I had to swallow my pride. It was time to go home.

Return to Rhode Island

My mother's apartment in Rhode Island was tiny, but it held more warmth than any place I'd lived before. She and my brother David squeezed me in, and suddenly I was transported back to childhood – the constant stream of visitors dropping by for cards and coffee, the familiar scent of my mother's cooking, the sound of friendly chatter filling every corner. It was exactly what I needed, though I didn't know it at the time.

Roger Williams Hospital became my second home. As a teaching hospital, it meant having a small army of physicians and residents attending to my case. I remember counting them once – ten medical professionals, all focused on getting me through the grueling six-day, round-the- clock IV drip of Cisplatin. I kept the sticker from that final bag of medicine – or poison, as I've come to think of it. That small adhesive label represents both the worst and, surprisingly, the best turning point of my life.

The Day Everything Changed

The side effects were brutal. One particularly violent reaction sent me back to the hospital, my eyes bloodshot from burst capillaries caused by endless bouts of vomiting. The cancer ward was full, so they placed me in the medical surgical floor. I was too exhausted to care where they put me – I just needed relief.

That's when she walked in.

Beth entered the room with quiet efficiency, but there was something in her presence that made the sterile hospital room feel different. Her dark hair was pulled back in a neat ponytail, and despite having already worked a twelve-hour shift, her eyes were alert and kind. She adjusted my IV with practiced hands, but it was the way she spoke to me – not as a patient, but as a person – that made my heart skip.

"Would you like to have dinner sometime?" The words tumbled out before I could stop them. To my surprise, she smiled and said yes.

Love During Treatment

We dated throughout my entire treatment. Beth saw me at my absolute worst – the endless rounds of nausea, the days when I couldn't lift my head from the pillow, the moments of fear I tried to hide. She never flinched. When I insisted on leaving the hospital at one in the morning after my final treatment, she came back after her twelve-hour shift to take me home. She knew I would try to leave on my own if she didn't.

The Long-Distance Challenge returning to Florida was necessary, but leaving Beth behind felt impossible. Her parents, especially her father Ted, were understandably concerned. Who falls in love with a sick man from another state? But Beth saw something beyond my illness, beyond the uncertainty. For six months, we maintained our relationship across the miles, with Beth making multiple trips to Florida despite everyone telling her she was crazy.

New Beginnings

The letter from my physician stated clearly that I would never be the same, but Beth saw possibilities where others saw limitations. When I found work in a warehouse, she supported me. When her father, a high school principal, suggested I take an aptitude test with his students, she encouraged me. That test led me to discover my passion for art, steering me toward a degree in Advertising Design at a school in South Florida.

Beth and I packed our modest belongings and moved to Fort Lauderdale. While I juggled work and classes, Beth took a position at a large hospital. We were building our future, saving for our wedding planned for October 7, 1988. For a high school dropout, making the Dean's list and joining the Perfection Club with a 4.0 GPA felt surreal. Beth celebrated every small victory with me, even stepping in to complete my final Fine Arts term paper when circumstances forced her to – but that's a story for another chapter.

Through it all, Beth showed me what true dedication looks like. Like her father, who devoted his life to education, Beth approached everything – her career, our relationship, our dreams – with unwavering commitment. Ted, thank you for both your blessing to marry your daughter and the guidance that helped me find my path. You showed me what real dedication looks like, a trait I see reflected every day in your daughter.

But even as we moved toward our wedding day, storm clouds were gathering on the horizon. The next chapter will reveal how addiction threatened to unravel everything we had built together, testing the bounds of Beth's dedication and our love in ways we never could have imagined.

CHAPTER 19

Bridge over Troubled Waters

Bridge over Troubled Waters
The neon sign of Tony's Pizza cast a harsh fluorescent glow across my brother David's face as he suddenly stood up from our table, his eyes fixed on an empty corner of the restaurant. "Leave me alone!" he shouted, his voice cracking with rage. "Just leave me alone!" My older brother and I watched helplessly as Dave berated our long- deceased father's image that only he could see. In that moment, I barely recognized the person before me – the same brother who had once been the coolest guy I knew, the one everyone in town wanted to be around.

Looking back, I realize that moment at Mario's was the beginning of the end, but David's story started long before that night – back in the late 70s and early 80s, when he was just another kid trying to find his way without a father.

The Coolest Guy in Town

David had a laugh that could fill a room, a deep, genuine rumble that made everyone around him want to join in. He was always easy to spot around town – his wild brown hair catching the wind as he hitchhiked from one end to the other, that confident stride that made even the bouncers at local bars forget to card him. While most kids our age were still asking permission to go to the movies, Dave was running with the older crowd, dating college girls, and living life like every day was an adventure.

But beneath that carefree exterior, Dave carried the same wound we all did – the loss of our father. The difference was how he chose to numb that pain. By eighteen, he had graduated from weekend beers to substances that should never have crossed his path. We didn't know then how that choice would alter the course of his life forever.

The Night Everything Changed

The call came sometime after midnight. Dave had been driving home – under the influence of what, we never knew for sure – when his car flipped on the stretch of road right in front of his apartment complex. The police couldn't find him at first; the impact had thrown him nearly forty feet from the vehicle. When they finally discovered him in the darkness, it seemed like a miracle he was alive at all. No broken bones, no major lacerations – just a small tear on his ear and an invisible injury that would change everything: a severe traumatic brain injury.

The hospital waiting room became our second home. Days blurred into weeks as Dave lay unresponsive, the steady beep of monitors the only indication he was still with us. The neurologist's words hung heavy in the air: "It's not likely he'll recover. He may never wake up."

So we prayed, our mother's rosary beads clicking softly in the fluorescent- lit hospital corridor.

We prayed harder when they said he'd never walk again.

We prayed through our tears when they said speech was unlikely. We prayed with hope when they said work would be impossible. And David? He proved them wrong. Every single time.

The Battle Behind the Miracle

Watching Dave relearn to walk was like watching a force of nature. He approached each physical therapy session with the same determination that had once made him the life of every party. His speech came back slowly – words slurring and stumbling at first, but growing stronger with each passing week. Within months, he was back at his government job, his recovery dubbed a miracle by the same doctors who had once offered such grim prognoses.

But the neurologist left us with one final warning, one that would prove devastatingly accurate: the part of Dave's brain that was injured needed time to heal, and any exposure to drugs or alcohol would derail that healing process completely.

For a while, it seemed like Dave understood the stakes. He attended his therapy sessions, took his medications, and stayed clean. But addiction doesn't listen to medical warnings, and neither did the "friends" who welcomed him back into their world with open arms and open bottles.

The Descent

Over the next five years, from 1982 through 1988, we watched helplessly as Dave slipped away from us. The recreational use became daily use. The prescribed medications mixed dangerously with street drugs. The paranoid schizophrenia that the doctors had warned about emerged like a shadow slowly darkening his mind. That night at Mario's Pizza wasn't an isolated incident. Dave's reality had become a frightening maze of voices and visions. Our family

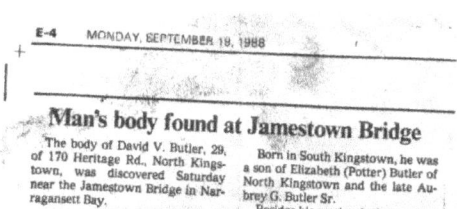

E-4   MONDAY, SEPTEMBER 19, 1988

Man's body found at Jamestown Bridge

The body of David V. Butler, 29, of 170 Heritage Rd., North Kingstown, was discovered Saturday near the Jamestown Bridge in Narragansett Bay.

Jamestown police said the body was sighted by a fisherman about 11:15 a.m., floating about 20 feet from the Jamestown shore. It did not appear the body had been in the water for a long time.

Police said they were awaiting autopsy results to determine the time, cause and circumstances of death.

Mr. Butler, a lifelong North Kingstown resident, was a welder for Electric Boat's submarine-building yard at Quonset Point.

Born in South Kingstown, he was a son of Elizabeth (Potter) Butler of North Kingstown and the late Aubrey G. Butler Sr.

Besides his mother he leaves four brothers, Aubrey G. Butler of Wakefield, Lloyd Butler of Coventry, Kenneth Butler in Florida and Robert Butler in North Carolina; and five sisters, Rosemary Case of West Warwick, Lois Fuscaldo and Norma Johnson, both of North Kingstown, Doris Crump in North Carolina and Barbara Stinnett in Ohio.

The funeral will be held Wednesday at 11 a.m. in the Lawrence E. Fagan Funeral Home, 825 Boston Neck Rd. Burial will be in Elm Grove Cemetery.

tried everything – interventions, Baker Acts, rehabilitation programs. But Dave had mastered the art of checking into rehab and checking out again, his compulsion to use stronger than any treatment program.

The medications meant to help him became another layer of sedation, dulling the bright spirit we'd once known. The Dave who could light up a room with his laugh became a stranger who fought invisible demons in pizza parlors and street corners.

Learning to Cope

Years later, I lay in bed one night, tears soaking my pillow as my wife Beth held me close. "Why can't I get over losing him?" I asked. "Every morning, no matter what good things are happening in my life, my first thought is of David."

Beth's answer changed everything: "You're not 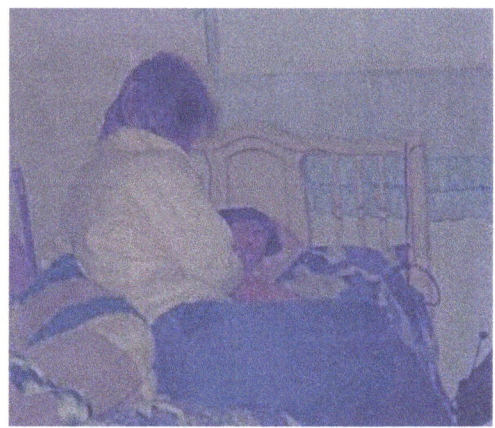 expected to get over the death of a sibling. You just have to learn new ways to cope."

Near the bridge where we lost Dave stands a lighthouse. I like to think it was the last thing he saw in this world – a beacon of light in his darkest moment. That's why I began creating lighthouse art on seashells, each one a tribute to my brother. When people ask why I don't sign them, I simply say, "If you know, you know." Each person who receives one has heard David's story, understanding that these aren't just decorative pieces – they're messages of hope and remembrance.

A Legacy of Loyalty

Dave was more than his struggles. He was the brother who would move mountains to help someone in need. As I often tell students when sharing his story, consider what he overcame: a near-fatal crash at sixty miles per hour, a forty-foot flight through the air, a coma, brain damage, partial paralysis, months of rehabilitation, and social ridicule. His will to live was extraordinary. The only force he couldn't overcome was addiction.

That's the cruel lottery of substance use – some can walk away, while others become trapped in a battle they never chose. Dave fought that battle with the same determination he'd shown in his recovery, but this time, the odds were stacked too high.

I've learned through David's example that family loyalty is everything. As I always say about my brother: "If you were against him, you could not win, but if you were with him, you could not lose." That loyalty lives on in the lighthouse shells I carve, in the stories I tell, and in the hope that by sharing his journey, others might find light in their own darkness.

For anyone who has lost a sibling, especially to suicide, know that you're not alone. The pain doesn't go away – nor should it – but it can transform. Find your lighthouse, whether it's art, writing, running, or something else entirely. Channel that energy that will never disappear into something that brings light to others.

In loving memory of our sweet and loving brother, David.
The coolest guy I ever knew. We all miss you very much.

*"Be honest with yourself and the window
to your life will be clear."*

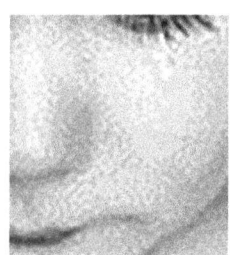

CHAPTER 20

Rise and Fall

The last time I saw my brother David alive, he was laughing at one of my terrible jokes, his eyes crinkling at the corners the way they always did. Three months later, his death devastated us all, leaving a void that none of us knew how to fill. Beth and I were living in Florida then, both working good jobs, finally settling into what looked like a normal life. For the first time, I didn't have to worry about food or shelter. I owned my home, had graduated from college, and landed a great job in advertising.

From the outside, everything seemed perfect.

But grief has a way of waiting for the quiet moments.

When you're surviving – moving from crisis to crisis, fighting cancer, building a career – you don't have time to process the weight you're carrying. It's only when you finally achieve some stability that your mind decides it's safe to unpack all the pain you've been storing away. For me, that moment came one ordinary morning when I couldn't take off my robe and go to work. Just couldn't do it. The heaviness in my limbs felt like concrete, and the thought of facing another day pretending everything was fine seemed impossible. I was thirty-three, but emotionally, I had hit a wall at the age of that scared six-year-old boy I used to be.

I took medical leave, started therapy through our insurance plan, and tried to understand what was happening to me. But sometimes, the breaking point comes in waves.

One night, after a sixteen-hour day in the advertising department of a retail store in Miami, I was walking to my car parked under the highway. The humid air clung to my skin as I passed a homeless man huddled against a concrete pillar. He was using newspapers as a blanket – newspapers containing three months of my hard work, my carefully designed ads that would disintegrate in the rain and wind. I stood there, frozen, watching my work quite literally being used as temporary shelter from the elements. Epiphany doesn't begin to describe what hit me in that moment.

Every sleepless night working on layouts, every careful font selection, every proud moment of seeing my work in print – it all felt hollow. After surviving cancer, I had promised myself I wouldn't waste a minute of my life. Yet here I was, pouring my energy into something that would literally dissolve in the next rainfall.

That night, Beth found me in our living room, still in my robe, shaking and crying. She sat with me, her medical training kicking in as she assessed my state. "You need help," she said quietly, her hand steady on my shoulder. "Real help, not just taking time off." Being married to a healthcare professional meant I couldn't hide behind vague explanations or brush off my symptoms. She saw through the facade I'd maintained for so long.

The therapist I found through our insurance seemed like a lifeline at first. But red flags started appearing: she talked more about her problems than listened to mine, shared inappropriate personal details, and then the unthinkable – she asked to borrow money. When she started using my credit card number to rent cars without my permission, Beth was furious. Her professional ethics as a healthcare worker made the betrayal even more egregious. She wanted to press charges, but I just wanted to retreat further into myself.

Drowning in what I thought was depression, and now dealing with the aftermath of a fraudulent therapist, I reached out to my older brother Gus. He had always been more than a brother – he'd stepped into the role of father figure after our dad died. That phone call, meant to be a lifeline in my darkness, turned into something else entirely.

"Ken," he said, his voice heavy with a secret he'd carried for decades, "there's something you need to know about Dad's death." He told me about going to identify the body, about finding the prescription drugs and alcohol bottles scattered throughout the apartment. The revelation that our father had likely taken his own life – whether intentionally or not – pushed me deeper into the abyss I was already fighting.

During my attempts at therapy, memories I'd long suppressed started surfacing. The trauma of childhood abuse, the reality of being molested – it all came rushing back. With my older brothers dealing with their own demons and not wanting to burden my younger brother, I reached out to a relative for help tracking down my abuser, hoping confrontation might bring healing. The response was simple: the man had drowned years ago. "The world has a way of weeding out the bad people," my brother-in-law said, but the knowledge brought little comfort.

Twenty years after that first failed attempt at therapy, I finally received an accurate diagnosis: PTSD. Not depression, though depression was certainly part of it. The relief of having a name for the chaos in my mind was overwhelming. For the first time, the path forward seemed clear, even if it wouldn't be easy.

Reflection

Recovery isn't linear, and it certainly isn't one-size-fits-all. Through my journey, I've learned several crucial truths about healing from trauma:

The right diagnosis changes everything. For years, I was treated for depression when PTSD was the underlying issue. It's like trying to fix a broken bone with cough medicine – the treatment simply can't work if the diagnosis is wrong. In today's world, we have resources our parents never had. We can research therapists, verify credentials, and demand proper care. Use these tools. The wrong therapist can do more harm than good, as I learned the hard way. Support comes in many forms, but professional help is irreplaceable. Some people turn exclusively to religion, support groups, or friends. While these can be valuable parts of recovery, they shouldn't be the only tools in your arsenal. True healing requires learning to stand on your own while accepting support from others. Professional therapy, when done right, teaches you how to self-motivate and cope, skills that stay with you even when external support isn't available.

Beth often reminds me that healing is about learning new ways to cope, not just managing symptoms. Some days are better than others. Most people who know me describe me as the most positive person they've ever met, but Beth sees the complexity beneath that positivity. She understands that my optimistic persona is both a coping mechanism and a genuine part of who I am.

Is it denial? Maybe sometimes. Is it fake? I don't think so. It's my way of choosing light over darkness, of using positivity as a tool rather than letting trauma define me. But now, with proper therapy and support, I'm learning to balance that positivity with authenticity, to acknowledge the hard days without letting them overwhelm me.

At fifty-eight, I'm finally doing the work I should have done at thirty-three. But healing doesn't have an expiration date. Whether you're carrying childhood trauma, battling PTSD, or dealing with any form of mental health struggle, it's never too late to start the journey toward healing. The key is finding the right help, building a strong support system, and committing to the process, no matter how long it takes.

Because in the end, we all just want to feel better. Until we address our core wounds, many of us will seek relief wherever we can find it — in substances, in work, in denial. I found my initial solace in writing, and now, finally, in proper therapy. It's hard work, facing decades of accumulated pain, but it's necessary work. No matter how strong you think you are, unresolved trauma will eventually demand to be heard.

The good news is, you don't have to face it alone. And you don't have to have it all figured out to start healing

"Wherever you go, there you are."

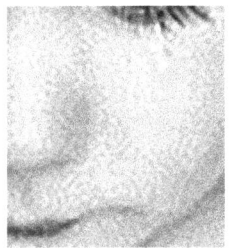

CHAPTER 21

Left a Good Job in the City Heading North

I used to sing along to "Proud Mary" on my drive to work in Coconut Creek, Florida, the lyrics hitting differently each time. Left a good job in the city, working for the man every night and day... I did have the best job in the world, but something was missing. The endless sunshine and comfortable routine couldn't fill the emptiness Beth and I felt. We wanted children.

The impact of cancer treatment years earlier had left me unable to have children naturally, a reality that took time to fully accept. Beth and I spent years trying to become parents, each attempt ending in disappointment. Before my second surgery and chemotherapy, my physician had suggested freezing sperm – a moment of foresight for which I'm forever grateful. We began the in-vitro fertilization process with hope, but the journey was more challenging than we could have imagined.

Beth endured countless hormone shots, her body and emotions riding a cruel roller coaster that mimicked pregnancy only to end in heartbreak. Each failed attempt felt like losing a child we'd never met. The financial cost was substantial, but the emotional toll was devastating. I remember holding Beth after our last failed attempt, both of us knowing it was time to stop but neither wanting to say the words first.

"Maybe we need to go home," Beth said one evening, as we sat on our back porch watching the Florida sunset. "If we're not going to be parents, let's at least be around family." The decision to leave Florida wasn't easy, but it felt right. We sold our home and moved to New Hampshire, bringing our Corvette and motorcycle with us. We planned trips, talked about early retirement – trying to convince ourselves that a life without children could still be fulfilling.

But the desire to be parents never faded. The conversation that changed everything happened on a quiet Sunday morning over coffee. I was still struggling with the idea of adoption, my mind stuck on the notion that being a father meant passing on my genes.

"Who had the most impact on your life?" Beth asked, setting down her coffee cup. "Master Kim, my Tae Kwon Do teacher," I answered without hesitation.

"He doesn't have a gene connection to you," she said, her eyes meeting mine, "and you love and respect him just as much as if he were related to you."

The simplicity and truth of her words hit me like a physical force. Master Kim had saved my life, shaped who I became, without sharing a single strand of DNA. In that moment, the path forward became clear – we would adopt from Korea. It felt like coming full circle, honoring the connection that had helped me survive my own darkest times.

The adoption process was intense, requiring more than $20,000 and endless paperwork. But nothing could prepare us for the moment EJ Butler came into our lives in 2000. I remember standing at the airport, my heart pounding as we waited. When they placed him in our arms, the years of longing and loss transformed into something beautiful. This tiny boy from Korea, with his curious eyes and gentle smile, was our son.

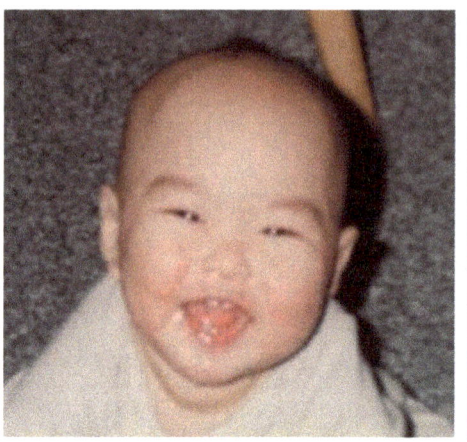 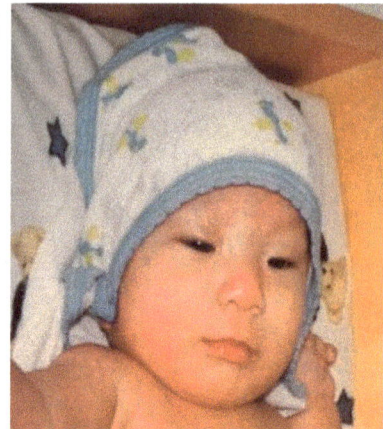

Life was transformed, but we still had one more journey to make. Rhode Island called us home, despite my reservations. and all the demons I'd run from years ago still lurked in the shadows of my hometown. But sometimes, healing requires facing what we fear most.

I threw myself into work at the YMCA, teaching Tae Kwon Do, managing the fitness center, and directing the after-school program. EJ attended preschool right there, and watching him grow in the same building where I helped other families felt like a kind of poetry. Beth noticed how EJ lit up around other children, and one evening she broached the subject of adopting again.

"He needs a sibling," she said, watching EJ play with his toys. "Our family isn't complete yet." The decision to adopt TY was easier – we knew the joy waiting on the other side of the paperwork and fees. When he arrived at four months old, our family circle widened again. Both boys attended the YMCA, and life settled into a beautiful rhythm.

But something stirred in me again. The YMCA had given me countless opportunities to help people in the community, but I felt called to explore corporate fitness. When a position opened with a large corporate wellness firm based in New York, managing an onsite wellness center at a Fortune 100 organization, it felt like the next right step. In March 2006, I started what I thought would be my dream job – helping employees get healthy in the middle of their workday.

I was three weeks into this new chapter when life reminded me of its unpredictability. In December 2005, my older brother Butch had died of a massive heart attack. Despite my own health and fitness, our family history of heart disease whispered warnings I couldn't ignore. As I scheduled a check-up, I thought about family – the ones we're born to, the ones we choose, and the ones we build. Each connection shapes us, genes or no genes.

Trust your instincts, Master Kim used to say, they are almost always correct. Mine had led me to Beth, to our sons, and to a life richer than I could have imagined when I first left that good job in the city.

CHAPTER 22

Serious as a Heart Attack

The fluorescent lights of the hospital lobby buzzed overhead as my legs gave out. My wife Beth's scream seemed to come from far away as I slumped against the cold tile wall, our two sons frozen in shock beside her. The world was closing in, my chest a vice grip that wouldn't release. This wasn't how I had imagined my story ending – not at forty-eight, not in front of my family, and certainly not after being told just ninety days earlier that I was in "superb condition." But let me back up.

In December 2005, my older brother died from a massive heart attack in his home. His death shook our family to its core and sent me on a mission to confirm my own health.

With our family history of heart disease looming like a shadow, I underwent every cardiac test available. The thallium stress test, EKG, blood work – you name it, I did it. I can still see the cardiologist's reassuring smile as he reviewed my results. "Mr. Butler, you are in superb condition for a forty-eight-year-old man," he said, leaning back in his leather office chair. "Everything is okay. You do have slightly elevated cholesterol, but we can correct that with Crestor."

I should have been relieved. After all, I was in the best shape of my life after seven years of work at the YMCA. My fighting weight was back to one hundred and eighty-five pounds, and I felt lean and ready for anything. I had just started my dream job two weeks earlier.

Then came that April night.

It was just past midnight on April 21, 2006, when I jolted awake, my lungs screaming for air. Living in a rural area, I knew calling EMS might mean the difference between life and death – and not in a good way. I shook Beth awake, my voice barely a whisper as I fought for breath. The fear in her eyes matched my own as she helped me to the car, our sons stumbling sleepily behind us.

The drive to the hospital remains a blur of panic and determination. I had to recline the passenger seat all the way back, literally rumbling my lungs to draw in whatever air I could get. Each breath was a battle, each mile a testament to Beth's steady hands on the wheel despite her terror.

Then came the lobby scene – my body giving out just steps from help, my family watching in horror as medical staff rushed to my aid. I survived, but the questions that followed were almost as painful as the heart attack itself.

The next day, as I lay in the cardiac unit being prepped for catheterization, I demanded answers. The conversation with my new cardiologist would change my understanding of health forever. "How can I be 'fine Mr. Butler' in January and practically die on my couch in April?" I asked, my voice hoarse from the intubation.

The doctor's response was both enlightening and terrifying. "Your descending main artery is 99 percent blocked," he said, showing me the images. "Think of it like a highway gradually narrowing to a single lane. The tests we did earlier would only show a 70 percent blockage or more – and most people don't survive that level of blockage for more than a few seconds." "Then how did I survive?"

His explanation was a cruel irony. "Your vigorous exercise habits created collateral arteries – think of them as back roads around the main highway. Without those alternate routes, you wouldn't be here having this conversation."

The reality was staggering. The very thing I had done to stay healthy – intense exercise – had masked a condition that nearly killed me. Now, I take sixteen daily medications to stay alive. My body, once my trusted ally, had become an uncertain companion.

The most frightening part? The only way to check for new blockages is through catheterization – considered a procedure, not a test. Insurance won't cover it unless it's an emergency, meaning I have to nearly die again to get checked. It's like walking through a minefield with a blindfold on.

I returned to work after twelve weeks of recovery, determined to adapt to my new normal. I changed my lifestyle even more, thinking I had finally figured things out. Then, a year later, came the Type II diabetes diagnosis – another reminder that health is never as simple as we want it to be.

Today, each breath is a gift, each heartbeat a reminder of both my mortality and my resilience. My family's fear during that night in the hospital lobby has transformed into a fierce vigilance – we face each day knowing that life can change in a heartbeat, but we face it together.

CHAPTER 23

Ticking Time Bomb

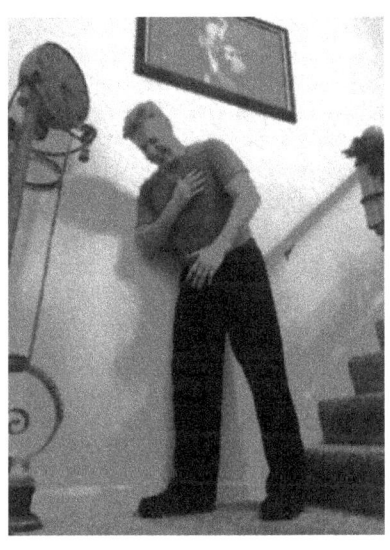

There I stood in my professional fitness studio, surrounded by certification plaques and client success photos, staring at my new medical chart. After fifteen years of helping others transform their bodies and twelve years of leading a my own world class wellness center, I was now diagnosed with Type II diabetes. The irony wasn't lost on me – the guy who could recite optimal blood sugar levels while designing workout plans was now struggling with his own.

The shadow of my father's early heart attacks had always loomed over me, but somehow I'd convinced myself that my lifestyle would protect me. I was wrong.

Being the "good patient" I'd never wanted to be, I attended diabetic training classes at the same hospital where I'd had my first heart attack six months earlier. The fluorescent lights and antiseptic smell reminded me that I was now straddling two worlds – fitness professional and cardiac patient.

Leaving the class that Wednesday afternoon, I felt the first pinch in my chest. As a trainer, I knew every warning sign of a cardiac event. As a man who prided himself on resilience, I chose to ignore them. I called Beth, my wife of twenty years, trying to sound casual.

"Hey, just letting you know I'm having some chest discomfort," I said, pacing outside the hospital entrance.

"Don't hesitate," Beth replied, her voice carrying that unique blend of exasperation and love I'd grown to depend on. "You're literally at a hospital. Walk back inside and ask for help." "You know how they get with my history," I argued, even as another pinch made me wince. "They'll admit me, run a thousand tests, and it'll turn out to be heartburn. Remember last time?"

"Fine," she sighed, knowing how stubborn I could be. "At least go to the doctor's office. It's right around the corner, and your primary care physician Dr. Martinez knows your history." Twenty years of marriage had taught me to recognize when Beth's practical nature was saving me from myself. I got in my car, each heartbeat feeling like a countdown timer.

The doctor's office staff took one look at my face and rushed me in. Within sixty seconds, I was in the exam room. Within ninety seconds, the room started spinning, and my professional facade crumbled. The last thing I heard before passing out was someone calling for nitroglycerin. I woke up back in the familiar cardiac unit, post-surgery, with two new stents and a humbling reality. The surgeon, Dr. Chen, stood at my bedside, shaking his head. "I'm not sure why you're alive," he said plainly, "and I'm certainly not sure how you were walking around with 99 percent blockage. Your fitness level probably saved your life, but it also masked how serious this was." The next six to eight weeks of recovery tested everything I believed about myself. The doctor's words echoed in my head: "Many people don't go back to work after this type of medical condition." But the thought of not returning to my studio felt like another kind of death. I modified my training approach, learned to listen to my body with the same attention I demanded from my clients, and gradually rebuilt my strength.

That year, I won awards for leadership and team building – accolades that meant more because they came after I learned to embrace both strength and vulnerability. My near-death experience had taught me that true fitness meant more than physical capability.

 The biggest change came in how we lived outside the gym. Beth and I looked at each other one night, both thinking about how close we'd come to losing everything, and decided to buy a camper. Our boys, EJ and TY, thought we'd lost our minds until that first weekend under the stars.

For the next four years, we became weekend warriors of a different sort. Instead of counting reps, we counted shooting stars. Rather than tracking heart rates on monitors, we measured time by sunsets and campfires. Every Friday after work, we'd pack up and head out, creating the kind of memories that no cardiac event could take away.

Looking back, my body had been a ticking time bomb, but that second brush with death hadn't been an ending – it had been a beginning. It taught our family that the most important reps were the ones that counted moments together, and the best kind of strength was built around a campfire, watching our boys grow up under an open sky.

CHAPTER 24

Riding Along in My Automobile

It was one of those perfect Memorial Day weekends in 2012 - the kind where the sun seems to polish everything it touches. 8:30 AM, and I was heading east on my usual route, thinking about getting home to Beth and the boys. Traffic flowed smoothly, everyone doing their part in the morning dance of commuting. The radio played softly. Just another morning. Until it wasn't.

In just five seconds, my world spun sideways:

I saw him drift across

the center line, his car aimed at mine like an arrow The impact hit - metal screaming against metal

Airbags exploded in my face, a cloud of chemical dust

My car spun around, now rolling backward at fifty-five MPH Somewhere in the chaos, I heard myself yell

He had crossed so far into my lane that he hit me on my right shoulder line. My car, now facing east but rolling backward, skidded fifty feet into oncoming traffic. When it finally stopped, smoke began curling from under the hood. My heart hammered against my ribs as I watched that smoke, thinking about all the action movies where cars explode. My fingers fumbled for my phone - not 911, but Beth. Always Beth first. "I've been in an accident," I managed to say when she answered. "The car's smoking. I can't get out." My voice sounded strange in my ears, higher than usual.

Then came a tap on my window - gentle, almost casual. The fire captain stood there, his face bearing that unique mix of concern and seen-it-all calm that first responders master.

"You alright in there?" he asked, his voice muffled through the glass. "Yes," I said, still gripping the phone. "But I can't get out."

He gave me a look that reminded me of my own father - patient, kind, with just a hint of 'bless your heart.' "Relax," he said, "and put your car in park."

Of course. The doors wouldn't open in drive. Such a simple thing, but in that moment, it felt like advanced calculus.

Beth arrived before the ambulance left. One look at her face, and I knew I wasn't waving off medical attention.

"Oh, you will get in that ambulance," she said, in that tone that brooked no argument. The same tone she used with our boys when safety was non-negotiable.

The immediate diagnosis was classic whiplash, but that was just the beginning. Over the next four years, the pain grew quietly, like ivy climbing a wall. Small adjustments became daily habits - the careful way I moved, the constant awareness of my back. Then came December 22, 2016: anterior and posterior lumbar fusion surgery. Four months of recovery followed, each day a reminder of how quickly life can change.

But the physical recovery wasn't the hardest part. It was the fear that lingered, that still lingers. Every time I drive, I find myself watching oncoming cars with a survivor's eyes, wondering if the next driver will be looking at their phone instead of the road. All my years of facing various challenges pale compared to this constant awareness that someone's casual decision to check a text could end everything.

A few weeks after the accident, my son and I were driving past the crash site. He'd been quiet, watching the spot approach through his window.

"Dad," he said finally, "why did you have to get hit?"

I looked at him in the rearview mirror, saw the real question in his eyes. In that moment, I wasn't just answering about the crash - I was teaching him about life, about making sense of the senseless.

"Maybe," I said carefully, "there was someone behind me that day - maybe a family with a small child, or an elderly person. Maybe God put me there to protect them." He thought about this, his face serious. "So you took the hit, right, Dad?"

"Yes, buddy," I said softly. "I took the hit."

That's why I'm sharing this story. Every day, drivers pick up their phones, thinking one quick check won't matter. But it does matter. That text, that social media update, that quick email response - none of it is worth destroying lives over. When you're behind the wheel, please remember my story. Remember that your momentary distraction could force someone else to "take the hit." Turn your phone off. Whatever message is waiting, I promise you - it can wait.

Reflection

Life speaks to us in whispers sometimes - that gut feeling, that small voice of instinct. That morning had tried to tell me something, suggested I change my plans. Now, I listen more carefully to those whispers. But I've also learned that sometimes, being in the wrong place at the right time means someone else gets to be in the right place after all. Sometimes, taking the hit is exactly where you're meant to be.

CHAPTER 25

Breath in, breath out

It was a perfect Saturday in June at dusk at the Jimmy Buffett concert. Beth and I swayed to the song breathe in, breathe out.

Her hand warm in mine, both of us laughing at the crowd's enthusiastic response. I remember thinking how gracefully she moved, even after twenty years of marriage. That was the last carefree weekend before everything changed.

Looking back, the signs had been there for months, maybe longer. Small things we dismissed or explained away. Beth would occasionally stumble, catching herself with a quiet laugh. "Just clumsy today," she'd say, but these moments were becoming more frequent. At night, she'd shift restlessly in bed, her legs refusing to settle. When she struggled to grip her coffee mug one morning, she simply switched to using her right hand instead of her left.

Beth's aunt had battled Multiple Sclerosis for years before passing away. Beth watched her uncle care for her with unwavering dedication, helping her navigate life from a wheelchair.

Sometimes, in quiet moments, I'd wondered if I possessed that kind of strength. It was the kind of thought you push away, never expecting to face it yourself.

The reality of what we'd been missing crashed into our lives during a casual girls' day at our home. Beth's friend Toni, who hadn't seen her in several months, watched Beth walk across the living room and immediately spoke up.

"Are you limping?" Toni asked, her voice carrying a note of concern that made everyone else in the room falls silent.

Beth attempted to brush it off. "I hurt my foot a while back. It's nothing."

"Have you been checked for MS?" Toni persisted, glancing meaningfully at Beth's uneven gait. That question launched us into weeks of medical limbo. Each test brought a new wave of anxiety. MRI machines hummed. Doctors spoke in carefully measured tones. Beth faced each appointment with quiet determination, while I felt myself struggling to breath every time we entered another medical building.

The confirmation of MS came on a sunny Tuesday in June 2014. The neurologist's office was almost painfully bright, sunlight streaming through wide windows as he delivered the news we'd been dreading. Beth reached for my hand; her grip strong despite everything we'd just learned. Telling our children was one of the hardest conversations we've ever had. We've always believed in being honest with them, but how do you explain that their mother's body is at war with itself? Beth found the words somehow, balancing truth with hope, while I struggled not to let my own fear show.

I didn't expect the diagnosis to hit me as hard as it did. While Beth showed incredible strength,

I found myself sinking into depression. It seemed selfish - Beth was the one facing this disease, yet I was the one who couldn't get out of bed some mornings. The weight of potential futures pressed down on me: Would I be strong enough to be what she needed? Could I match her uncle's devotion?

Therapy helped me understand that my reaction wasn't selfishness - it was a normal response to trauma. Spouses of those diagnosed with chronic illnesses often experience their own form of grief and fear. Learning this didn't immediately lift the depression, but it helped me face it with less shame.

Through it all, Beth has remained my anchor. She handles her symptoms with quiet grace, though I know there are moments when she's terrified. We're learning to navigate this new reality together, taking each day as it comes. Sometimes we still catch ourselves remembering that carefree couple at the Jimmy Buffett concert, but we're writing a different story now - one of resilience, love, and facing the unknown hand in hand.

This time, I experienced another mental health crisis. My history with PTSD is insidious. The treatment focused on how to cope with a spouse diagnosed with a serious illness. Beth had always taken care of me through everything—cancer, heart attacks, depression, diabetes, an auto accident, and day-to-day support. Now I felt helpless in every single aspect of supporting her in her time of need, which only deepened my depression.

I felt sadness for my wife, then I felt bad that I was getting depressed, and the cycle went round and round until I sought professional help again. I had sought counseling before, but that experience had left its own scars—the therapist had taken advantage of my good nature, using my credit for personal purposes. So many things had just gotten pushed down even further.

With so much buried beneath the surface, I finally received the correct diagnosis. I am not simply depressed; I have finally been properly diagnosed and treated for posttraumatic stress disorder. I chose to be transparent about my medical diagnosis for two important reasons.

First, I have nothing to hide. This is the real issue in our society—we hide these things as if they were our fault. No more shame for me and no more hiding. I view these medical records as proof of the battles that I am most proud of overcoming.

Second, in recent history, there have been some very dishonest people who have fabricated stories about mental health struggles. That dishonesty marginalizes the real fighters and survivors—both those who are struggling through crisis and the highly functioning individuals living with mental illness.

I continue to learn new ways to cope. Somehow, all of my experiences have prepared me for this moment: to take care of my wife. Beth has taken care of me throughout our marriage, and she has prepared me well to handle caring for her. It is true that what doesn't kill you makes you stronger. Although my wife is doing great now, the threat of MS is always there, a shadow we've learned to cope with. Our defense is positive offense. We keep the faith.

Me and PTSD

This time, the treatment focused on how to cope with a spouse that is diagnosed with a serious illness. Beth always took care of me. Cancer, heart attacks, depression, diabetes, auto accident, and day-to-day support. Now I felt helpless in every single aspect of supporting her in her time of need. That of course made me more depressed that I somehow focused on me and then the spiral began. I felt bad for my wife, then I felt bad that I was getting depressed, and the cycle went round and round until I sought professional help again. As you recall, I had at one point sought counseling. The therapist took advantage of me and my good nature, borrowed money, and used my credit card for personal purposes. So there really were many things that had just gotten pushed down even further.

With so much buried beneath the surface, I finally received the correct diagnosis. I am not depressed, I have finally been properly diagnosed and treated with posttraumatic stress disorder. I chose to illustrate the records on my medical diagnosis because of two reasons. First, I have nothing to hide. In fact, this is the issue in our society. We simply hide these things as if it were our fault. No more shame for me and no more hiding. I view these documents as proof of the battles that I am most proud of.

Second, in recent history, there have been some very dishonest and despicable people in the world that have written about things that are just fiction. That dishonesty marginalizes the real fighters and survivors that are down and out, dealing with a crisis and the highly functioning individuals with mental illness.

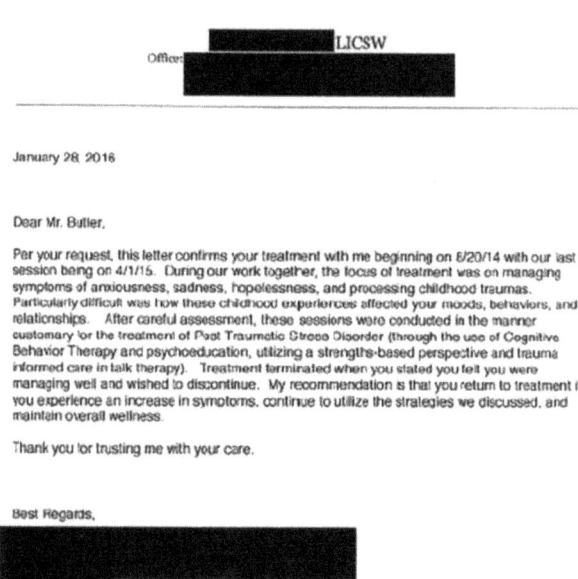

LICSW

Office:

January 28, 2016

Dear Mr. Butler,

Per your request, this letter confirms your treatment with me beginning on 8/20/14 with our last session being on 4/1/15. During our work together, the focus of treatment was on managing symptoms of anxiousness, sadness, hopelessness, and processing childhood traumas. Particularly difficult was how these childhood experiences affected your moods, behaviors, and relationships. After careful assessment, these sessions were conducted in the manner customary for the treatment of Post Traumatic Stress Disorder (through the use of Cognitive Behavior Therapy and psychoeducation, utilizing a strengths-based perspective and trauma informed care in talk therapy). Treatment terminated when you stated you felt you were managing well and wished to discontinue. My recommendation is that you return to treatment if you experience an increase in symptoms, continue to utilize the strategies we discussed, and maintain overall wellness.

Thank you for trusting me with your care.

Best Regards,

LICSW

CHAPTER 26

Stent Man

I began to gain weight, experiencing the all-too-familiar warning signs. I'd been down this road before: difficult sleeping, crippling fatigue, looking and feeling increasingly unhealthy.

One night, I started coughing uncontrollably, suddenly unable to breathe. The only way to describe it was like drowning on dry land.

After eleven stents between 2006 and 2018, you'd think doctors would have realized my treatment wasn't working. Despite medication, diet, and exercise, the blockages kept coming. This time was different, though. I wasn't driving myself to the hospital. My family witnessed me in full-blown congestive heart failure. When the ambulance arrived, the paramedics rushed me to the hospital.

I'd been to the catheterization lab so many times that the staff joked and called me "stent man." Thirteen stents from 2006 to 2018. While recovering in the hospital, I woke up to see a whiteboard with three letters in big red marker: "CHF PATIENT." I lay there alone, with no explanation from doctors or nurses.

The next day, after my thirteenth stent was installed, the doctors conducted their grand rounds. I knew something fundamental wasn't working with my treatment. During rounds, a resident asked me a question that would change everything: "Have you ever been tested to see if your body responds to the prescribed medication designed to help fight off clots?"

When I said no, they suggested a test. Just forty-five minutes later, they delivered the news— I'd been on the wrong medicine. My cardiologist switched my medication after twelve long years.

Finally, I was on medication actually designed to prevent my specific type of blockages.

My sons, now in their early twenties, saw me in this condition, probably frightened in a way that could never be undone. Both my children and my wife were with me during my first heart attack—the time I drove myself, which was probably not the best idea. They've watched me struggle time after time with blockages, culminating in thirteen stents.

I'm still not sure why I'm the one who survives or how I've been blessed to endure such terrible things. But as I always say, "If you get sick, you better be healthy."

CHAPTER 28

Fighting the Invisible Battle

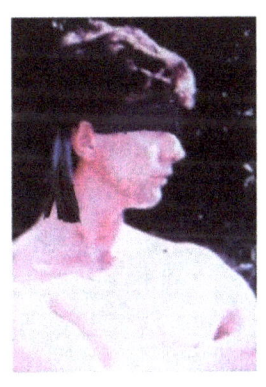

"You have scleroderma diffuse," the rheumatologist said after months of testing. The words hung in the air as I tried to process what this meant for my future. After surviving multiple heart issues, I now faced an entirely new battle.

It began in April 2019. Just when I thought my heart problems were behind me, my body started sending warning signals. Fatigue crept in slowly at first, then became overwhelming. Dizziness made everyday tasks challenging. Something was wrong, but what?

For months, doctors pointed to my heart—the logical culprit given my history. Test after test followed: echocardiograms, stress tests, bloodwork. Each one came back ruling out cardiac issues. The mystery deepened while my symptoms worsened. My hands began to lose their strength. Simple tasks like opening jars or gripping my motorcycle's handlebars became difficult. Finally, a referral to rheumatology revealed the answer. Scleroderma diffuse—a rare autoimmune disease affecting roughly 25,000 Americans, predominantly women. This wasn't just any diagnosis; it was considered the most severe subset, with potential five-year mortality rates that made my heart sink.

"What exactly is happening to my body?" I asked the specialist.

Scleroderma attacks from within and without. The disease causes the body to produce too much collagen, hardening the skin until it becomes tight and shiny. Internally, it can damage vital organs—heart, lungs, kidneys, intestines. The small red spots appearing on my face were telltale signs. My joints ached constantly. The potential complications were terrifying: pulmonary hypertension, kidney failure, cardiac involvement.

Beth, my wife and personal nurse, held my hand as we absorbed the news. Her eyes showed concern, but her voice remained steady as she asked about treatment options. Throughout our marriage, she had stood beside me through heart problems, back surgery, mental health challenges—never wavering in her belief that we would overcome whatever came our way. When the doctor mentioned weekly injections of methotrexate—essentially chemotherapy— Beth simply nodded and said, "I'll learn how to administer them."

That evening at home, the weight of the diagnosis fully hit me. I sat on our porch watching the sunset, my motorcycle gleaming in the driveway. Would I ever ride again? Would I see my grandchildren grow up? The questions swirled as darkness fell.

Beth joined me, placing a cup of tea in my hands. "One day at a time," she whispered, knowing no grand promises could be made.

The treatment began immediately. Methotrexate injections every week, with Beth carefully administering each dose. The medication carried its own risks—it could only be taken for two years before potentially damaging major organs. A double-edged sword that might save me while threatening me in different ways.

All of this unfolded as COVID-19 swept across the world. In an unexpected blessing, my employer allowed me to work remotely. On my worst days, when fatigue made even sitting at a desk challenging, I could take short breaks without scrutiny. The pandemic that brought tragedy to so many offered me the flexibility I desperately needed.

Family became my lifeline during this period. My brother, ever the comedian, responded to my diagnosis with typical sibling humor: "So you're telling me you have a girl disease?" His irreverence made me laugh when I most needed it. My sons visited more frequently, helping with household tasks that had become difficult. Nieces and nephews called regularly, their youthful energy contagious even through phone lines.

As months passed, small victories emerged. The disease progression slowed. The medication, despite its harsh side effects, seemed to be working. I began to approach the all- important five- year survival mark—that critical milestone when statistical odds shift dramatically in favor of long-term survival.

But some losses were inevitable. My declining grip strength and coordination made motorcycle riding increasingly dangerous. For someone who had been riding since age 14, this was more than losing a hobby—it was surrendering a piece of my identity.

I decided my beloved bike, a dream machine my wife had gifted me for my 50th birthday, needed a new owner. Before selling it, I planned one final ride. Early on a crisp morning, I set out on familiar roads, feeling the rumble beneath me and the wind against my face.

Each curve and straightaway became a meditation. I wasn't angry about what scleroderma was taking from me; instead, I felt profound gratitude for the decades of freedom two wheels had provided. That last ride wasn't a funeral—it was a celebration of all the miles behind me. As I pulled into our driveway hours later, Beth was waiting. She knew what this moment meant without words being needed. She simply handed me a glass of water and said, "Good ride?" "The best," I replied, my heart full despite the loss.

Now, as I approach March 22, 2024—my five-year milestone with scleroderma—I reflect on all that has brought me to this point. The disease has not progressed as aggressively as initially feared. While I've lost some physical capabilities, I've gained perspective that only comes through confronting mortality repeatedly.

Through heart failure, back surgery, mental health struggles, and now an autoimmune disease, I've learned that physical resilience begins with emotional and spiritual strength. Being honest with myself about limitations while refusing to be defined by them has been crucial.

My experiences have crystallized into values that guide me daily:

- **Be honest with yourself** about what you can and cannot control.
- **Maintain your physical health** even when you're feeling well—it creates reserves for when illness strikes.
- **Trust selectively** but deeply, building relationships that withstand life's storms.
- **Stay active in whatever ways your body allows**—movement is medicine.
- **Nurture your spiritual life**, finding meaning beyond physical circumstances.
- **Stand independently** while knowing when to seek professional help.
- **Choose friends carefully**, investing in relationships that bring mutual growth.
- **Help others daily**, even in small ways—service provides perspective.
- **Work continuously to master your emotions** rather than letting them master you.
- **Be your own advocate** in medical situations while respecting expertise.

If you know someone struggling—with addiction, relationship problems, health issues— reach out. Say something. Do something. I've survived because people didn't remain silent when I needed help, even when I didn't realize I needed it.

Of all the lessons I've learned, perhaps the most important is this: faith, hope, and positivity aren't just pleasant sentiments—they're survival tools. They've saved my life repeatedly, carrying me through moments when medical science reached its limits.

As I write this chapter of my life, I encourage you to examine your own story. What values sustain you when challenges arise? What principles guide your decisions? Write them down. Review them often. Let them shape who you become.

Life will bring storms to everyone. The question isn't whether difficulties will come, but how we'll weather them when they do. Build your foundation now, brick by brick, value by value. Then, when the winds blow—and they will—you'll stand firm, perhaps bent but unbroken.

Family Reflections

I was deeply inspired by my siblings to write and publish this book, and I wanted to include the thoughts of my living siblings. This image was captured at a family reunion hosted by my brother Robert in North Carolina.

The shared thoughts below are poignant, and I admire the strength it takes to share them.

In Loving Memory
Gus – RIP
Rosemary – RIP
Butch – RIP
Dave – RIP

Words from My Siblings

Lois shares:

"If you can't fly, then run; if you can't run, then walk; if you can't walk, then crawl. But whatever you do, you have to keep moving forward." Ken: I feel like I've been doing this most of my life.

Norma shares:

"Growing up in the Butler home was dysfunctional, violent, and traumatic. However, with the love and strength of our mom and the bond we shared as siblings, we learned to stand strong and become survivors—not victims. We lived then and live now by Mom's words: 'Keep the Faith.'"

Doris shares:

"No matter how tough life gets, we always have each other to lean on, and I feel very blessed.

Many people aren't that fortunate. Mom gave us the love and strength to survive anything life throws our way. United we stand, divided we fall."

Ken shares:
"Big Boys Do Cry."

Robert shares:
"Big boys don't cry, but grown men do."

Ken: Thank you, brother!

Barbara shares:
"We are more than survivors. We are the phoenix that rises from the ashes."

David Butler:
"If you are with us, you can't lose,
If you are against us, you can't win."

The End

About the Author

An accomplished martial artist, graphic artist, poet, personal trainer, and registered clergy with experience related to the topic of domestic violence. He is well-respected among his peers for his tenacity to survive anything that comes his way including serious medical conditions, family trage- dies, depression, PTSD, auto accidents, and more. He is the recipient of multiple community service awards for outstanding services to several communities from RI to **Ken Butler** Florida. He is recognized as a leader in the wellness industry and has won awards that celebrate his leadership and team building capac- ities. Being the eighth sibling of ten children that was raised by a single mom only ignited his passion for creativity and determination that is truly remarkable. He often says, "Be your own hero." He cer- tainly is considered a hero by so many individuals from all walks of life that he impacted through his inspiring relationships, teachings, and insights.

www.ingramcontent.com/pod-product-compliance
Lightning Source LLC
Chambersburg PA
CBHW051215120626
46547CB00013B/1356